ACCOMMODATION AND CLEANING SERVICES

Volume 2: Management

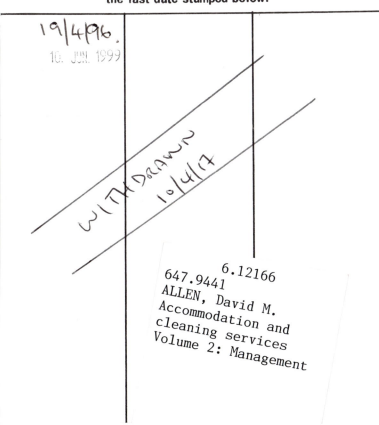
David M. Allen

ecturer in Applied Science
titute of Higher Education

**LEWS CASTLE COLLEGE
OF FURTHER EDUCATION**

LIBREX

HUTCHINSON

uckland   Johannesburg

Hutchinson Education

An imprint of Century Hutchinson Ltd,
62−65 Chandos Place, London WC2N 4NW

Century Hutchinson Australia Pty Ltd
89−91 Albion Street, Surry Hills,
New South Wales 2010, Australia

Century Hutchinson New Zealand Limited
PO Box 40−086, Glenfield, Auckland 10, New Zealand

Century Hutchinson South Africa (Pty) Ltd
PO Box 337, Bergvlei 2012, South Africa

First published 1983
Reprinted 1984, 1986, 1988

Set in Times

Printed and bound in Great Britain by
Anchor Brendon Ltd, Tiptree, Essex

British Library Cataloguing in Publication Data
Allen, David
    Accommodation and cleaning services
    Vol. 2: Management
    1. Hotel management   2. Hotels, taverns, etc. −
    Great Britain   3. Buildings − Cleaning
    I. Title
    647′.9441′068   TX910.G7

ISBN 0 09 151001 5

Contents

Foreword

By Lord Parry of Neyland

David Allen is a leader among a small group of academics who, earlier than so many of their colleagues in teaching, have realised that Britain earns its living as much from the so-called 'service sector' of the economy as from manufacturing goods.

Working in an area where heavy industry created so much of the social structure and founded and funded so much of the further education system he has, nevertheless, associated himself and his courses with the less popular but vital areas of research. In consequence he has become an important student of Britain's cleaning industry. His book carries the authority of its author's experience.

As chairman of the Wales Tourist Board and a member of the British Tourist Authority, President of the British Institute of Cleaning Science and, temporarily, Chairman of the emerging Council of the cleaning industry, I have worked with David Allen on the obviously related interests that make tourism on the one hand and cleaning on the other vital contributors to Britain's rapidly changing economy.

Cleanliness is not only next to Godliness, but it is, in fact, the key to a better living for Britain. We have deluded ourselves for too long that our heavy industrial economy would continue to pay our country's way. It has failed to do that for more years than we have been prepared to admit. The service sector of the economy has long been responsible for closing the gap and, on occasions, has actually created a balance of payments surplus for Britain in its overseas markets. For example, the tourism industry and the cleaning industry earn similar sums of money for Britain overseas and save similar sums of money for Britain at home, circulating it moreover through the home financial system. Together, they earned more money than the offshore oil industry did for Britain last year.

This book and its companion volume recognize that the considerable level of technical and management skills required by supervisors and managers in the accommodation service sector of the hospitality industry and in the cleaning industry are the key to Britain's economic survival. These technical skills are basic to the industry's efficiency and to its growing confidence.

It is vital that not only industry, but those servicing it, be seen to be the key workers of the future. Qualifications and competence will be essential in achieving this.

David Allen's book has come out at exactly the right time to achieve it.

Preface

This book and its companion volume on operations were written to meet the requirements of students studying accommodation and cleaning services and who are enrolled on the following courses.

TEC Diploma in Hotel Catering and Institutional Operations
HND and TEC Higher Diplomas in Hotel Catering and Institutional Management
HCIMA Parts A and B
CGLI 764 Cleaning Science
CGLI 708 Accommodation Services

The books will also be of particular value to supervisors and managers involved in the provision of accommodation and cleaning services in the following areas:

Hospital Domestic Services Departments
Contract Cleaning Companies
Housekeeping Departments in Hotels and Residential Establishments
Public Authority Buildings

Taken as a whole the various organizations companies, establishments and institutions involved in the provision and supply of accommodation and cleaning services form one of the largest industries in the UK with an annual turnover of several billion pounds. The supervisor or manager in any of the various sectors of the industry must have a depth and spread of technical knowledge and be conversant with and be able to exercise a wide range of general and particular supervisory and management techniques in order to deal with the often complex interrelating factors involved in determining the services required in a particular situation and in providing these services. The student must acquire that knowledge and become conversant with these techniques and skills.

Only within recent years has it been recognized that the supervisor or manager of accommodation services requires an extraordinary range of knowledge, skills, techniques and abilities. This is reflected in the very limited information available dealing objectively and critically with technical matters and with the supervisory and management techniques particular to accommodation and cleaning services. This book and its companion volume were written in response to that lack of information.

In preparing both volumes of this work it has been the intention to provide students of accommodation services and in-post supervisors and managers with the necessary knowledge of technical matters relevant to the various services, with the necessary practical details relevant to each service, with a knowledge of the factors determining the types and standard of service to be provided and with a knowledge of particular supervisory and management techniques relevant to accommodation services. Only with a comprehensive understanding of all aspects of accommodation services is it possible to objectively determine, plan and control the types and standard of services required in any particular situation.

It is inevitable that some points in the text will be controversial and that there are some broad generalizations. However, wherever possible the validity of factors judged to be controversial have been tested under laboratory or working conditions and broad generalizations have been used where a detailed treatment would have rendered the subject all but incomprehensible to other than the most experienced manager.

The preparation of this book would not have been possible without the support of my wife Mary. For her help and for putting up with more than one might reasonably expect, I express my gratitude. I also thank Mrs Doreen Evans and her colleagues for their help in the preparation of the text and my colleagues and students without whose help and criticism it would not have been possible.

Separately I wish to extend my thanks to Mrs G. M. Hayes for her contribution in the preparation of the sections dealing with Bedding and Linen, Interior Design, Hygiene and Pest Control in Volume 1 and for contribution in the initial drafting of the various chapters in this volume.

Acknowledgements

I wish to thank the British Standards Institution for permission to reproduce, in modified form, copyright material from BS 5378 and BS 5499. I also wish to thank the following for their assistance in the preparation of photographs for inclusion in this work: Mrs E. Johnson; Doncaster Metropolitan Institute of Higher Education; Danum Hotel, Doncaster.

1 Introduction

Volume 1 was concerned largely with the material finishes, furniture, fixtures and fittings of a building, the equipment and chemicals used in the cleaning and maintenance of fabric, furniture and furnishings of a building, the range of services comprising accommodation services, the practical aspects involved in providing these services and the factors determining the types, extent and standards of service required by an establishment.

This volume describes the services required or supplied by various types of organization, the administrative structure of these services and the duties of personnel employed within them; safety requirements; techniques and methods of work planning, costing and control.

It must be pointed out that this book deals with supervisory and management skills particular to accommodation and cleaning services and does not deal in detail with the more general areas, for example, of personnel supervision and management which are dealt with comprehensively by numerous other books.

The organization of accommodation and cleaning services is concerned with the precise specification of work to be carried out in order to meet the particular requirements of an establishment and with the deployment of labour, materials and equipment in the most cost-effective combination in order to carry out that work and provide the standard of service required. Once the resources available have been deployed it then becomes necessary to control the standard of work carried out, largely through effective monitoring of the usage of labour, equipment and materials.

2 Organization and personnel

Services associated with the cleaning and maintenance of a building and with the comfort of the occupants will be required by virtually every type of organization. In 1981 it is estimated that £3 billion was spent in Britain on cleaning services of which approximately 10% was spent on materials and equipment.

This chapter outlines the organizational structure of the major users and suppliers of accommodation and cleaning services, the types of service they provide and the principal duties of the staff providing those services.

The principal users and suppliers are hospitals, hotels, residential establishments, local authorities and contract cleaning companies. The principal services provided by staff will be cleaning and maintenance although they may also be involved in linen, food and beverage and laundry services.

Hospital domestic services

Organization

The structure of the National Health Service (post-reorganization in 1982) is shown in Figure 1, and Figures 2 and 3 show the organization of domestic services management in hospitals.

Services

The function of the domestic services department (DSD) in a hospital is to provide, organize and control an effective cleaning service for the whole of the hospital, i.e. wards, theatre areas, out-patients, laboratories, specialist, e.g. remedial, departments, gymnasia, offices, staff facilities, patients' recreational areas and residences. In some hospitals, the department may also be responsible for the cleaning of the catering department. However, this normally comes within the jurisdiction of the catering manager. The work of the department is primarily cleaning, with the aim of producing a technically clean, aesthetically pleasing environment, which will:

1 Assist in promoting the comfort of patients, visitors and staff.
2 Contribute to the health care of the patient by using cleaning procedures which will control harmful organisms and help to prevent the spread of infection.
3 Contribute to the maintenance of the fabric of the building.

Although the cleaning of residences, offices and general areas can be scheduled to be unobtrusive, i.e. when these areas are least used, the work in the patient areas is carried out around the patients. The methods of work chosen must therefore be quiet, fast and efficient and disturb the patients as little as possible. This also means that the domestic staff who work on patient areas must be of a temperament that can cope with working among sick people.

The provision of linen and laundry services is normally the responsibility of the laundry manager and his/her department.

Duties of DSD personnel

Domestic services manager (DSM) The DSM is the head of the department. The principal duties are:

1 *Staffing,* including recruitment, training, disciplining and maintenance of personnel records for the department.
2 *Planning* to ensure that the department will provide necessary services in the future.

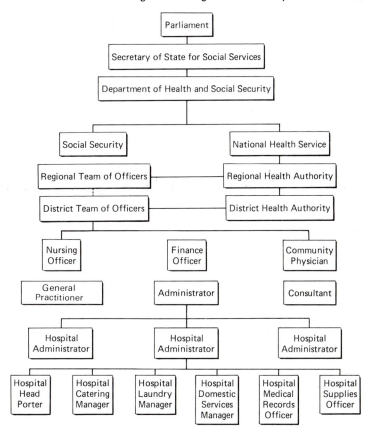

Figure 1 *Structure of the National Health Service*

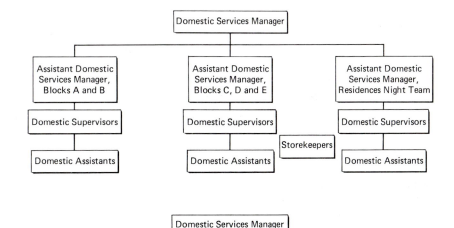

Figure 2
Organization chart for domestic services in a large hospital

Figure 3 *Organization chart for domestic services in a small hospital*

3   *Organizing* the work of the assistant DSMs or domestic supervisors to ensure that the department is run smoothly on a day-to-day basis.
4   *Controlling* the work of the department, e.g. standards and budgets.
5   *Participating* in decision-making regarding future developments, e.g. commissioning new buildings, control of infection, budgetary requirements, staffing requirements.
6   *Liaising* with consumers of the service provided, i.e. staff and patients, to ensure that the required service is achieved.
7   *Record keeping,* including control data, personnel records and training records.

Assistant DSM(s)   Deputizes for the DSM over the full range of duties in a large hospital or in a small hospital has sole responsibility for the department. He will be responsible for planning, organizing and controlling the daily work load of domestic supervisors responsible to him.

Where there is more than one assistant DSM, duties may be allocated in a variety of ways, for example:

1   ADSM A   Blocks A–D
    ADSM B   Blocks F–G

2   ADSM A   Day shift
    ADSM B   Afternoon twilight shift
    ADSM C   Night shift

3   ADSM 1   Training
    ADSM 2   In-patient areas
    ADSM 3   Out-patient department
                  and residences

Domestic supervisor(s)   Responsible for the daily planning, organization and control of a group of domestic assistants. The recommended maximum number of domestic assistants per supervisor is 20 full-time equivalents. Generally the hospital will be divided into geographical areas with a supervisor per shift responsible for the staff and their work in that area. Where there is a large supervisory team, there will often be a new supervisor who is still undergoing training, who will act as a relief supervisor and deputize for

other supervisors in their absence. Occasionally, in a very small unit, the domestic supervisor may be the most senior member of the department. Where this is the case, such a person will normally be responsible to a DSM in a larger unit. Some large departments may employ their own domestic storekeeperes, who will be responsible for the ordering, issuing and control of domestic stores and equipment. Where this grade does not exist, this work is usually carried out by the domestic supervisors.

Domestic assistants   Responsible for actually carrying out the various cleaning tasks. Many hospitals allocate trained, experienced domestic assistants to one job which they perform each time they are on duty, e.g. a floor maintenance team, and a relief team of staff carries out any work that becomes available because of sickness, holidays, etc., of the regular members of staff. Frequently, the relief team will be composed of new members of staff who are still receiving training. The duties of the domestic assistant cover the work carried out by those grades of staff formerly known as cleaners and maids and much of the work which used to be carried out by ward orderlies.

Hotels

Within hotels, the cleaning and domestic services are provided by the housekeeping department.

Organization

Figures 4 and 5 show the organization structure for a large and a small hotel. Figure 6 shows the structure of a housekeeping department.

Services

The function of the hotel housekeeping department is to provide, organize and control the cleaning, linen, laundry and room servicing throughout the hotel. The standard of this work and particularly the type and amount of room servicing provided will depend upon the level of

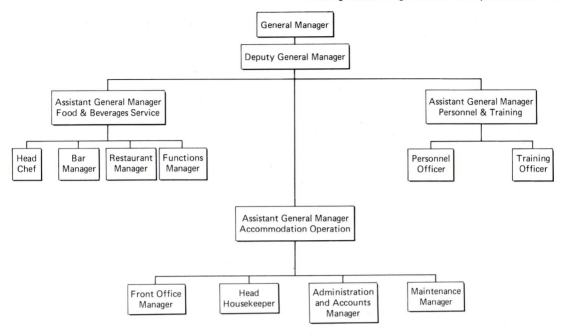

Figure 4 *Organization chart for a large hotel*

Figure 5 *Organization chart for a small hotel*

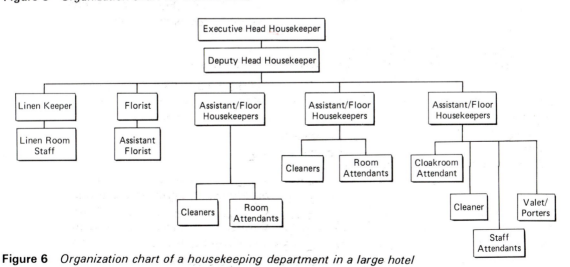

Figure 6 *Organization chart of a housekeeping department in a large hotel*

accommodation provided. The provision of these services will be reflected in the tariff for each room or added to the guest's account. The aims of this department are:

1 To provide these services economically and efficiently.
2 To promote the comfort of the guest, staff and visitors.
3 To assist in the maintenance of the fabric of the building, whilst contributing to a safe, healthy environment.

The department will also be required to provide those 'finishing' touches which will increase a guest's enjoyment of his stay at an hotel, e.g. floral arrangements, personal laundry/dry-cleaning service and hotel literature.

The only form of catering with which the department will normally be involved is the provision of early morning tea and sometimes the service of Continental breakfasts when these are taken in the guest's room.

Duties of staff

Head or executive housekeeper This post exists in large hotels and the head or executive housekeeper will be responsible for a number of assistant housekeepers. The principal duties of this post are:

1 *Staffing* which will include recruitment, training, discipline and welfare.
2 *Planning* to ensure that future needs of the hotel can be met.
3 *Organizing* the work of the department including the preparation of work schedules and rotas.
4 *Supervising* the work of his/her assistants to ensure the department runs efficiently.
5 *Controlling* the work of the department, e.g. standards and budgets.
6 *Advising* the general manager of the future budgetary and organizational needs of the department.
7 *Liaising* with other departments (see Figure 7).
8 *Preparation and keeping* of records, reports, wages sheets.

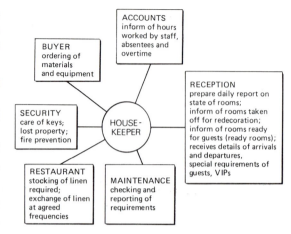

Figure 7 *Duties of a housekeeper involving other departments*

Deputy head housekeeper This post exists in very large hotels. He/she will deputize for the head housekeeper over the full range of duties. Frequently the head housekeeper and deputy will work separate shifts with an overlap period in the middle of the day.

Assistant or floor housekeeper An hotel will usually be divided geographically into units, often by floors, and each unit will be supervised by an assistant housekeeper, also known as the floor housekeeper. This person organizes and supervises the housekeeping service provided on the unit, as delegated by the head or deputy head housekeeper.

Linen keeper Responsible to the head housekeeper for the provision and control of linen services in the hotel. This will include not only bed linen and table linen, but also staff uniforms and soft furnishings. Where the linen is owned by the hotel, the linen keeper may be responsible for the supervision of linen room assistants but, where the hotel hires its linen, it may only be necessary for one person to work in this area, as the linen hire firm will carry out many of the procedures traditionally carried out by hotel staff, e.g. mending.

Florist Traditionally many large hotels employed their own florist, and possibly assistant florists, who were responsible to the head housekeeper for all floral displays in the hotel. Now, for reasons of cost, many hotels contract the supply of floral decorations to a local florist or a specialist firm. Only very large or luxury hotels still employ their own florist.

Room maids are responsible for the servicing of guests' bedrooms, private sitting rooms and bathrooms. This will include bed-making, cleaning. linen exchange, and possibly turning down and room service. An individual maid will generally be responsible for the servicing of 10 to 15 rooms.

Staff maids are another group of staff responsible to the assistant or floor housekeeper. Their main duties are the cleaning and servicing of staff living and recreational accommodation.

Cleaners This group of staff, also responsible to an assistant or floor housekeeper, is responsible for the cleaning of public rooms, shared bathroom facilities, ladies cloakroom and staff accommodation such as offices, storerooms and corridors. This general cleaning work is sometimes undertaken by a contract cleaning firm.

Cloakroom attendants are employed in some hotels to look after ladies cloakroom facilities. Some hotels employ a member of staff on a full-time basis for this post, but many employ part-time staff only when necessary, e.g. large functions.

Valet/porters Traditionally a valet was employed by most first-class hotels, his function being to care for the wardrobe of male guests. Nowadays, because of general change of habits, a valet will rarely be employed by a hotel, instead a valet/porter may be found in some first-class hotels. His duties combine those of attending to the wardrobe of male guests with those of a houseporter, e.g. high-level cleaning and assisting with the removal of furniture.

Residential establishments

Residential establishments include students' halls of residence or hostels belonging to universities, polytechnics and institutes of higher education, adult education centres, staff colleges, training centres and residential homes and schools run by local authorities or other organizations. The head of such establishments may be called the bursar, the domestic bursar, the steward, the residence manager, the hall manager, or the matron.

Organization

A variety of organization structures exist. Figure 8 shows the traditional structure of a residential establishment and Figure 9 the organization of domestic services in a university where a residence manager is responsible for several establishments.

Services

Traditionally, student hostels have provided a full catering service and a full cleaning service for residents during term time and relied upon vacations to provide the opportunity for staff to carry out periodic cleaning and maintenance. Increasingly, because of the need to provide moderately priced accommodation for residents, many halls offer the student a simplified catering service and provide small kitchens which they share, together with reduced cleaning and servicing of bedrooms. Some of the latest designs of halls are of the self-catering variety, where there are no catering services provided, and where the accommodation and cleaning services are only provided to communal areas and to study bedrooms before their occupation.

A further change in the use of many halls of residence occurs during vacations when many educational establishments seek full occupancy of their residences and try to achieve this by letting them as conference, holiday and leisure accommodation. This increased use of halls and hostels contributes to their economic viability and may result in the need for greater flexibility in styles and standards of service.

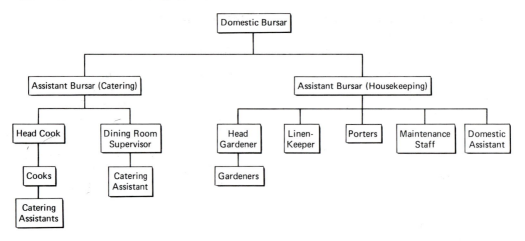

Figure 8 *Organization chart of a residential establishment*

A member of the academic staff, usually known as the warden, will normally be responsible for the welfare and discipline of residents.

In residential homes and schools run by local authorities and other organizations a full range of catering, cleaning and associated services is usually provided.

Duties of staff

Domestic Bursar Responsible for the organization and control of all aspects of the services provided including catering, cleaning and maintenance of the grounds in which the establishment is set. Duties will vary from one establishment to another but specifically they will include:

- Budgetary control.
- Staff recruitment and discipline.
- Staff training and welfare.
- Establishment and maintenance of standards of service.
- Preparation of work schedules and rotas.
- Reporting and checking of maintenance requirements.
- Control of gardening and maintenance staff.

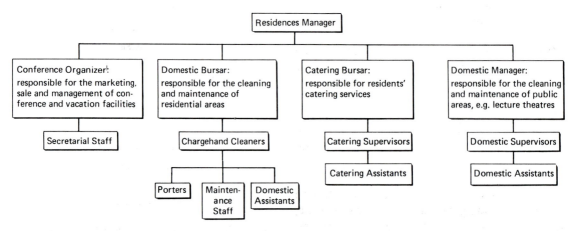

Figure 9 *Organization structure of hostels in one university*

- Control of laundry and linen room.
- Control of kitchen staff.
- Ordering of food, cleaning equipment and materials, and linen.
- Care of lost property.
- Security, including the care of keys.
- Fire precautions.
- Stock control.
- Provision of advice and reports with respect to staffing and finance.
- Conference organizer.

Residence manager   Responsible for the management of all residences within an establishment and the person to whom a conference organizer, domestic and catering bursars and domestic managers will be responsible.

Assistant bursars may be employed to assist and deputize for the domestic bursar over the full range of duties, or, alternatively, the assistant may be given specific responsibilities, e.g. the provision of the catering service, and also deputize during the absence of the domestic bursar. The number of assistant bursars in any establishment will be determined by the size of the residence and the standard of services to be undertaken.

Domestic assistants   Responsible to the assistant bursar for the performance of accommodation services and cleaning procedures.

Maintenance staff   Responsible for any building and equipment maintenance, often including the fuelling of central heating systems.

Porters will usually be responsible for the security of a hostel, high cleaning procedures and assistance with the removal of heavy furniture, fittings and residents' luggage.

Gardeners   As many residences have extensive grounds, including gardens and sports facilities, there will usually be a team of gardeners and groundsmen to ensure their maintenance.

Local government

Organization

There is generally no overall responsibility for the provision of cleaning and accommodation services in a local authority. The director of a division or department will be responsible for services within his department. Typical organization charts are shown in Figure 10 for an education and a social services department with reference to schools and residential homes.

Services

Local government is involved in a wide range of activities, and so the provision of cleaning and accommodation services must be appropriate to each type of establishment and the type of activities carried out within it. In some authorities contractors will undertake the provision of cleaning services.

Offices   In addition to the usual type of office accommodation it will include council chambers and conference rooms. Particular problems encountered will include:

1   Older premises which may have particularly

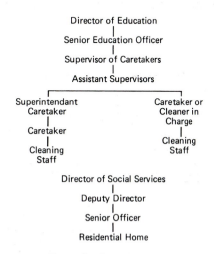

Figure 10 *Organization of local government departments*

high ceilings and may have been decorated to very high standards.

2 Limited provision of lifts which can make the moving of equipment difficult.

3 Changes in use at short notice which affect cleaning schedules.

Cleaning, maintenance and security will usually be supervised by a caretaker.

Schools will include classrooms, laboratories, sports halls, changing rooms, pottery and art rooms, domestic science kitchens, swimming pools and dining areas. Particular problems include:

1 Extensive use of building during days and evenings.

2 Sandwiching of work periods between periods of building usage.

3 Vandalism and extensive soilage of many facilities.

4 Age and design of some schools.

Cleaning, maintenance and security will usually be supervised by a caretaker (who may be resident).

Residential establishments In addition to many of the facilities found in hospitals, hotels and hostels, this type of accommodation will include classrooms, medical therapy areas, workshops, recreational areas, sports halls and changing rooms. Such establishments are usually concerned with the care of the elderly or children. Particular problems include:

1 Building occupied at all times.

2 Residents may be mentally, physically or socially handicapped and may present the accommodation and cleaning services staff with a variety of problems, e.g. immobility, hyperactivity, incontinence.

Accommodation and cleaning services will usually be supervised or managed by a resident warden, domestic bursar or matron.

Museums, art galleries, libraries and archives These establishments will include display areas, exhibits, workshops, archive areas for old documents and/or books and extensive shelving carrying books. Particular problems include:

1 Dust control and control of ultra-violet light necessary to prevent the deterioration of exhibits.

2 Cleaning of extensive numbers of shelves, books and areas of glass.

The organization and supervision of cleaning and maintenance usually forms part of the curator's or librarian's job description. The cleaning of technical areas and exhibits is normally undertaken by curatorial staff and by cleaning staff under their supervision.

Public toilets are frequently subjected to heavy soilage and vandalism. Routine cleaning is undertaken by an attendant.

Sports and leisure centres will include squash courts, gymnasia, swimming pools, restaurants and bars, indoor bowling greens and sport courts. Particular problems will include:

1 Extensive usage during day and evening.

2 Need to maintain the floors of gymnasia and squash courts.

3 High standard of hygiene required in wet areas.

4 Maintenance of air and water conditioning plant.

Cleaning services will be organized and managed by the centre manager.

Duties of caretakers

Duties vary from one authority to another and from one establishment to another, but will usually include:

● Liaison with other staff and departments.

● Employment and dismissal of operatives.

● Staff training and welfare.

● Preparation of work schedules and rotas.

- Maintenance of established cleaning standards.
- Reporting and checking of maintenance requirements.
- Practical involvement in cleaning and maintenance tasks.
- Boiler firing and heating systems.
- Care of lost property
- Security, including the care of keys.
- Ordering of cleaning materials and equipment.
- Stock control.

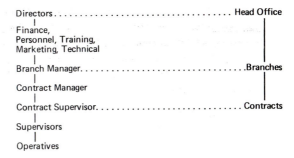

Figure 11 *Organization chart of a contract cleaning company*

Contract cleaning

Organization

The contract cleaning industry consists of a small number of large companies, a larger number of medium-sized companies and numerous small ones. Some larger companies are also involved in the supply and manufacture of cleaning equipment and materials. The actual organization of a company varies greatly but for larger companies that shown in Figure 11 is typical.

Head office will be responsible for the formation of policy, training and the overall direction of the company. Branch managers and contract supervisors are frequently recruited from personnel with previous experience in accommodation and cleaning services in hotels, halls of residence and hospitals. Each branch is usually fairly independent and is often responsible for all aspects of a contract. When large contracts are undertaken, one branch may consist of one contract. Contract supervisors may be responsible for one large contract or several smaller ones.

Services

Contract cleaners provide a range of general and specialized cleaning services which can be used by any organization requiring cleaning and servicing. Their services will generally include:

1   General cleaning of public rooms, wards, toilets and kitchens; provision of bedroom cleaning services.

2   Specialist cleaning and maintenance of clean areas.

3   Periodic cleaning of walls, ceilings, carpets, upholstery, windows.

In addition to cleaning, they may also provide a range of associated services, e.g. food and beverage services, linen supply.

The services of contract cleaners will be used in two broad types of situation:

1   To carry out general accommodation and cleaning services where management considers that the use of a specialized company will be more economic, management and staff do not have sufficient expertise and/or it is preferable not to be responsible for the day-to-day administration of this aspect of their activities.

2   To carry out specialized or periodic cleaning tasks where specialized skills and equipment are unavailable and it is uneconomical to teach staff specialized skills or purchase specialized equipment.

When a contractor undertakes work it will usually be on one of two bases:

a   With responsibility for all aspects of the service provided, which will include labour costs, equipment purchase and repair, purchase of all cleaning materials and supplies.

b   With responsibility for managerial and supervisory functions only. All labour, equipment and materials costs will still be borne directly by the client.

In either case, services will be provided on the basis of a negotiated and then fixed price.

The role of the supervisor in accommodation management

The posts within accommodation and cleaning services departments usually designated as supervisory level are:

Hotels: Assistant or Floor Housekeeper.
Hospitals: Domestic Supervisor.
Residential establishments: Assistant Domestic Bursar or Cleaning Supervisor.
Local government: Assistant Bursar, Superintendent Caretaker, Caretaker or Cleaner in Charge.
Contract cleaning: Contract Supervisor.

The function of a supervisor is the same in any industry, only the knowledge skills and conditions required to carry out that function vary, not only from industry to industry, but also from establishment to establishment within an industry. The supervisor is responsible to a manager and often assistant managers for planning, organizing and controlling the work of a group of staff, and for the leadership of that group of staff. The manager will be responsible for the setting of objectives and the forward planning, organizing and controlling of the department necessary to meet those objectives. The manager usually delegates to the supervisors the task of implementing these plans on a day-to-day basis. Supervisors must plan, organize and control the work of their groups of staff and provide leadership for their staff to ensure that the planned work is accomplished. Within accommodation and cleaning services departments, the manager should set the standard of service to be provided and allocate staff, equipment and materials to each area of work. The supervisor is the person who must make the most effective use of those resources to achieve the correct standard of work.

Planning

The accommodation manager should agree the objectives of the department, i.e. identify the areas to be cleaned and serviced and establish the standard of service to be provided to meet consumer requirements, and then allocate staff, materials and equipment to each area requiring servicing. Each group of staff will be responsible to a supervisor who understands the established standards and has been trained in the skills necessary to achieve those standards.

Supervisors must plan to use the resources of staff, materials and equipment efficiently and economically. The amount of decision-making in which supervisors are involved varies tremendously between the sectors of this industry. In some organizations standard methods of work for every cleaning and servicing procedure will have been agreed as company policy, whilst in others, the supervisor may be allocated an area to be cleaned and maintained but may be expected to decide upon the methods to be used and their implementation.

Organizing

Having planned how to use resources effectively to achieve the required service, the supervisor must organize their use. The supervisor's aim should be to ensure that skilled staff arrive at the correct place at the correct time with the necessary materials and equipment to carry out the work satisfactorily. If resources are not coordinated in this way, time will be wasted whilst staff wait for necessary equipment and materials, or equipment and materials will be lying idle until staff arrive, both of which are inefficient use of resources. Each job to be carried out requires careful coordination of these three interdependent resources.

Supervisors will rarely be involved in the actual selection and purchase of materials and equipment, but they will be the people required to put these items into operation, and so, should ensure that they advise the department manager of the performance of all materials and equipment and put forward well argued suggestions for improvements in future purchases. It is, therefore, necessary for supervisors to keep abreast of new developments in cleaning technology. The other area where supervisors may be involved in the organization of equipment and materials is in the ordering and issuing of the most appropriate items for any work to be undertaken, and to be prepared to make changes in methods of work where equipment and materials have to be altered for any reason.

It is vital that supervisors be flexible in their approach to their jobs and be prepared to react to changes in products, equipment, methods or required service and make any necessary provisions for their efficient use. It is also preferable for supervisors to try to predict the need for such changes and plan to meet them, rather than to be forced into making decisions when a change occurs.

The supervisor's role in the organization of staff will include staff training, to ensure that staff have the skills necessary to carry out the work, and allocation of work to each member of staff, to ensure that all necessary work is carried out and that each member of staff has a fair work load.

Training

Supervisors are generally involved with the following types of training:

Induction training to familiarize new members of staff with their place of work. It will assist them to settle in to the working routine and help them become accustomed to the requirements of their new job. The induction programme should include:

1 An introduction to the organization as a whole and its policies on timekeeping, hours of work, absenteeism, holidays, meal times, smoking, unions, pay, incentive schemes, sick pay, pensions, health and safety.
2 Their department and its relationship to other departments.
3 The place of work, including staff facilities.
4 Their role within the department, including

Staff member								
Job	Training date	Proficiency	Training date	Proficiency	Training date	Proficiency	Training date	Proficiency
Suction cleaning								
Damp mopping								
Upholstery								

Figure 12 *Example of part of a training schedule*

their duties, which should be provided in a written job description.
5 Other staff with whom they will work and to whom they will be responsible.

The programme may also include an element of training in the basic skills they will require and which will be continued in on-the-job training. A training schedule (see Figure 12) should be prepared, indicating the skills to be taught.

On-the-job training Supervisors participate in training courses held within their place of work. This usually involves training staff in the acquisition of specialist skills.

Off-the-job training Supervisors will rarely be involved as trainers in these training schemes which will normally be held away from the workplace, e.g. day-release courses at a local college of further education or block release course at the company training school. These courses usually involve the development of specialist skills. Supervisors will, however, be involved in the re-allocation of work of any members of their staff who are attending these courses.

Staff development Supervisors should be sufficiently aware of their staffing needs and the needs of their employing organization to be able to identify staff who require further training or refresher courses in specific skills and those who have the potential for promotion and should be trained in the skills necessary for such promotion. Supervisors must also plan to provide training to enable their staff to cope with changes in equipment, materials and methods of work.

The planning of staff training programmes will usually be carried out by the departmental manager and/or the personnel and training department, whilst the implementation of the programme will usually be the responsibility of the supervisor.

Work allocation

The degree of involvement of the supervisor in work allocation varies from organization to organization and will range from the preparation of duty and holiday rotas on a weekly or monthly basis, and the daily delegation of duties to staff based on these rotas, to merely delegating duties daily as staff arrive on duty from rotas previously drawn up by the departmental manager.

Supervisory staff in accommodation and cleaning services are rarely responsible for staff recruitment, which is usually carried out by the departmental manager. However, supervisors are sometimes included in the interviewing and selection stages of recruitment and must, therefore, be able to advise on the type of person most suitable for a particular vacancy.

Controlling

The first stage of control, the establishment of standards, will be the responsibility of the departmental manager, whilst the second and third stages will involve the supervisory grades. The second stage is the measurement of the end product of the work being carried out and its comparison with established standards. The third stage involves taking corrective action where necessary to ensure that the established standards are achieved in the future.

The measurement of the quality standards in accommodation and cleaning services depart-

ments can be difficult, often being the supervisor's subjective assessment of how the standard of the work in hand compares with an informed idea of what the established standard of work should be.

The measurement of the cost of the provision of the cleaning and servicing of an area can be exact and can be derived from assigning a cost to staff, materials, equipment and overheads for each job and comparing that cost with the predicted cost.

If, in the third stage of control, corrective action needs to be taken, it is essential that the supervisor has up-to-date cost control information and that quality control checks are carried out frequently. Even the subjectivity of quality control can be reduced by regularly training supervisors to recognize and achieve standards and by providing a quality control and inspection procedure, e.g. a checklist detailing the content of the work to be inspected.

Where the measurement of the work achieved highlights the need for remedial action, it is essential that such action is taken immediately, if it is to be effective. However, it is also necessary for the supervisor to understand how the problem has arisen so that the most appropriate course of action can be determined. If the cost of providing the service is too high, this may be due to wastage of either materials, equipment or manpower. If poor workmanship is evident, this may be due to the need for greater staff motivation, inspection or discipline, variations in the quality of materials and equipment provided or unforseen variations in the working routine, e.g. emergency doctors' rounds interrupting routines, extra work caused by an office party, or accidents in the school craftroom. If the correct standards are to be achieved, supervisors must train their staff and must inform them of what is expected of them and of how their performance compares with these expectations. This information must be communicated effectively to staff by their supervisors so that all members of staff can understand precisely what is required and know whether they are meeting these requirements. Where these requirements have been discussed and agreed with the staff, they are more likely to be accepted and achieved.

The ability to communicate effectively with both management and staff is essential if supervisors are to carry out their work satisfactorily.

Leading

When supervisors are appointed to their posts, they are automatically placed in positions of leadership. The very nature of the job places this authority upon them. When staff are selected for supervisory posts, it is preferable if one of the factors affecting their selection is that they possess qualities of leadership.

Leadership

Definition of this quality presents difficulties because of the problem of isolating common factors in the personalities of those who have it. When a group of people forms, it has needs, which demand someone who can influence or direct the group in the fulfilment of those needs, i.e. a leader. As the needs of the group change, so will the requirements of leadership change. One person may not fulfil the role of leader in every situation, e.g. a member of the group may be the leader in arranging social activities, another may act as leader of the work activities and another may act as leader in times of crisis or dispute. Consequently, it is often considered that leadership is the ability to influence and direct the activities of a group of people and that it is a personal attribute rather than something which can be learned.

When staff are promoted to supervisory grades, it is particularly helpful if the new supervisor has previously taken the role of leader in the work group and has positively contributed to that group as this helps in the group's acceptance of the new supervisor.

Supervisors must put into practice many of these qualities of leadership if they are to perform their duties satisfactorily. Supervisory training should therefore include courses on the development and use of all qualities of leadership.

If groups require leaders to help them satisfy

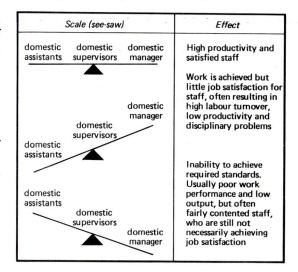

Scale (see-saw)	Effect
domestic assistants — domestic supervisors — domestic manager	High productivity and satisfied staff
domestic manager; domestic supervisors; domestic assistants	Work is achieved but little job satisfaction for staff, often resulting in high labour turnover, low productivity and disciplinary problems
domestic assistants; domestic supervisors; domestic manager	Inability to achieve required standards. Usually poor work performance and low output, but often fairly contented staff, who are still not necessarily achieving job satisfaction

Figure 13 *The see-saw effect*

their needs then supervisors must try to understand and help staff achieve their needs if they are to achieve a high output of satisfactory work. Supervisors must also fulfil the needs of their employers, which are easier to identify through job descriptions, staff training and regular contact with the departmental manager. They must try to balance these two sets of needs – see Figure 13.

Needs of staff will vary from individual to individual and from group to group. Supervisors should try to identify the needs of each individual member of the workforce and, also, relate those needs to the needs of that person within the working group, as the group may impose different needs upon the individual. Generally, human needs and the order of priority (after Maslow) are considered to be:

1 Physical needs, e.g. food, shelter, clothing.
2 Security needs, e.g. protection from danger, the long-term provision of physical needs.
3 Social needs, e.g. affection, a sense of belonging.
4 Need for recognition, e.g. self-esteem, status.
5 Need for self-fulfilment, e.g. responsibility, development, a sense of accomplishment.

Table 1 *Summary of the responsibilities of supervisors in various sectors of accommodation and cleaning services*

| Responsibility | Sector | | | | |
	Contract cleaners	Hospitals	Hotels	Local authorities	Residential establishments
Departmental forward planning, organization and control	Occas.	Rarely	Rarely	Freq.	Freq.
Day-to-day planning, organization and control	Always	Always	Always	Always	Always
Establishment of standards:	Occas.	Rarely	Rarely	Occas.	Occas.
Survey	Occas.	Rarely	Rarely	Occas.	Occas.
Specification	Occas.	Rarely	Rarely	Occas.	Occas.
Schedule	Occas.	Rarely	Rarely	Occas.	Occas.
Costing	Occas.	Never	Rarely	Occas.	Occas.
Maintenance of standards	Always	Always	Always	Always	Always
Stock purchase:	Occas.	Never	Rarely	Freq.	Occas.
Storage	Freq.	Freq.	Freq.	Freq.	Freq.
Issue	Freq.	Freq.	Freq.	Freq.	Freq.
Control	Always	Always	Always	Always	Always
Staffing:					
Recruitment	Freq.	Never	Rarely	Occas.	Rarely
Interview only	Occas.	Occas.	Freq.	Freq.	Freq.
Training:					
Induction	Always	Always	Always	Always	Always
On-the-job	Freq.	Freq.	Freq.	Freq.	Freq.
Discipline:					
Dismissal	Occas.	Never	Never	Never	Never
Written warning	Occas.	Never	Never	Rarely	Rarely
Verbal warning	Freq.	Freq.	Occas.	Freq.	Freq.
Industrial relations	Always	Always	Always	Always	Always
Health, safety, welfare	Always	Always	Always	Always	Always
Leadership	Always	Always	Always	Always	Always
Interior design	Never	Never	Occas.	Occas.	Occas.
Specialized procedures	Freq.	Always	Occas.	Occas.	Freq.
Catering	Never	Occas.	Occas.	Occas.	Freq.
Work study	Always	Always	Always	Always	Always
Incentive bonus schemes	Freq.	Freq.	Occas.	Occas.	Occas.
Maintenance of grounds or gardens	Occas.	Never	Never	Always	Always
Heating services	Rarely	Rarely	Rarely	Always	Freq.
Security	Freq.	Freq.	Always	Always	Always

It is important that accommodation and cleaning services supervisors do not make assumptions about their staff's needs, but rather assess which needs have to be fulfilled to provide each member of staff with job satisfaction. This should enable the supervisor to know what will motivate that person to work efficiently and consequently lead to high work performance. For example, if the supervisor assumes that domestic assistant A only works to earn money, whereas domestic assistant B needs not only money but also has social needs and the need for recognition, the supervisor may offer that member of staff extra wages in the form of overtime or bonus payments as a method of motivating her and of producing better quality work, when in fact, the inclusion of that person in a congenial team and the recognition of her worth to the department may produce better results.

Health, safety and welfare A supervisor should try to ensure that staff have a safe, healthy working environment and and welfare facilities.

Summary of the knowledge supervisors in accommodation (see Table 1)

- An understanding of the contribution of accommodation and cleaning services to the organization in which they work.
- Technical knowledge and skills – the nature of soil, cleaning equipment, cleaning agents, protective finishes, materials, fixtures and fittings, cleaning and servicing procedures.
- Supervisory skills – planning, organizing, controlling, leading.
- The ability to communicate effectively.
- Legal requirements – health, safety, welfare, industrial relations and their application.
- The ability to develop more efficient methods of work.

Health, safety and welfare

The maintenance of an environment that is safe in all respects and which is pleasant for both accommodation and cleaning services staff and for the users of a building is of paramount importance. To this end both employers and employees are obliged to maintain a building and adopt working practices and procedures which will actively promote the general health, safety and welfare of the users of a building.

Aspects of legislation

When determining policies for the health, safety and welfare of both staff and visitors to the workplace it is necessary to observe the relevant legislation, which is outlined in the following section.

Health and Safety at Work etc. Act 1974

This Act aims to provide a comprehensive piece of legislation dealing with the health, safety and welfare of all staff. It is a broad, generalized piece of legislation which does not lay down every detail of health, safety and welfare. Rather it is an 'enabling' Act, i.e. it authorizes the Secretary of State for Employment, through the Health and Safety Commission, to draw up detailed regulations and codes of practice on specific health and safety matters.

Legal obligations of employers These are as follows:

- To ensure, as far as practicable, the health, safety and welfare of all staff. To understand the full significance of this obligation, it must be appreciated that failure to comply with this obligation may result in a criminal prosecution and conviction even if no accident has taken place.
- To provide and maintain plant and systems of work that are safe and without risk to health. This includes not only tools and machinery, but also safety equipment and clothing.
- To make arrangements for safety in use, handling, storage and transport of articles and substances, whether solid, liquid or in the form of gas or vapour.
- To provide information, instruction, training and supervision as required to ensure the health and safety of all staff.
- To maintain premises in a safe and healthy condition. This includes entrances, exits and even vehicles.
- To provide a safe and healthy working environment, with adequate facilities and arrangements for staff welfare.
- To provide a written statement.

The written statement In almost every case an employer must provide a written statement of his general policy covering the health and safety at work of all staff and defining the organization and arrangements in force for carrying out that policy. It is not necessary to supply every member of staff with a personal copy of the statement. It is acceptable to display one copy on the staff notice board and/or to place a note in each employee's wage packet, telling him where he can see a copy of it.

Guidelines to the content of the policy statement are issued by the Health and Safety Commission. The main contents are:

1   A broad, general statement of intent signed by the managing director or equivalent, stating

the name of the person responsible for health and safety matters, emphasizing that the statement will be subject to regular review.

2 An explanation of the organization for health and safety matters showing:
the role of line managers
the role of specialists
the role of safety representatives and committees (these are normally required)
the role of individuals
the resources set aside for health, safety and welfare matters.

Legal obligations of employees These are as follows:

- To take reasonable care for the health and safety of himself and of other persons who may be affected by his acts or omissions at work.
- To co-operate with his employer as far as is necessary to meet or comply with any duty or requirement concerning health and safety.
- Not to interfere with or misuse anything provided in the interests of health, safety and welfare.

In addition, the Act enables safety representatives to be established in organizations where there is a recognized, independent trade union and so, employees may have duties in this capacity.

The National Insurance (Industrial Injuries) Act 1965 (amended by the Social Security Act 1975)

This act covers all employees and provides benefit for anyone who sustains personal injury, disease or death in the course of employment. If an employer is proved to have been negligent, and injuries result, the injured party may claim damages from the employer within three years of the injury's occurence.

Factories Act 1961

Briefly, amongst much else, this Act requires the guarding of machinery, the supply of lighting and heating to certain standards; the provision of toilet

and washing facilities and covers many other general aspects of health and safety.

Employers Liability (Defective Equipment) Act 1961

Should any member of staff suffer injury from a defect in any equipment supplied by an employer, the employer is deemed to be 'negligent' and can be sued. Having paid any damages or compensation awarded the employer may in turn sue the supplier involved.

Employers' Liability (Compulsory Insurance) Act 1969

Employers are obliged to carry a minimum insurance cover of £2 million for any one accident and to display their insurance certificate on the premises. Any failure to take out this insurance results in a fine of up to £200 and a further £50 for failure to display the certificate.

Occupiers' Liability Act 1957

This Act makes an employer responsible for the care of all visitors to his establishment. Failure to take such care may result in the payment of compensation to the sufferer.

Offices, Shops and Railway Premises Act 1963

This Act also applies to any premises open to members of the public for the sale of food and drink for immediate consumption. The more important provisions for health and safety of staff are outlined below.

- Premises, furniture and fittings must be kept clean. Floors and steps must be washed, or if it is effective, swept only.
- No overcrowding must occur. A minimum of 3.7 m² of floor space is required per person.
- Temperatures must be reasonable. A thermometer must be hung on each floor so that staff can check it. The temperature must reach 16°C within one hour of work commencing.

- Adequate ventilation must be provided.
- Lighting must be effective and adequate. All windows must be clean and free from obstruction.
- Sanitary provisions must be made and WCs kept clean, well maintained and provided with suitable lighting and ventilation.
- Washing facilities, including hot and cold running water, soap and drying facilities must be provided.
- Drinking water must be available for staff.
- Accommodation must be provided for staff clothing, not worn at work.
- Seats should be provided for staff who can use them without interference with their work.
- All floors, stairs, steps and passages must be maintained and free from obstruction. Handrails must be provided on staircases.
- Dangerous machinery must be properly fenced and users must be fully instructed in the dangers and safety precautions to be observed. Staff below the age of 18 years are not allowed to clean such machinery if this exposes them to risk of injury from a working part of the machine.
- A first-aid box or cupboard carrying the name of the person in charge of the box must be provided. A trained first-aider is required if there are 150 or more employees.

Food and Drugs Act 1955

The aim of this Act is to provide a pure and wholesome food supply for consumers. It is prohibited to sell food for human consumption which:

- Has been made injurious by the addition or subtraction of substances or by any treatment.
- Is not of the nature, substance or quality, e.g. inferior food, required.
- Has false or misleading labelling or advertising.
- Is unfit, e.g. decomposed or contaminated.

The Act provides for the punishment of persons found guilty of offences under the Act. An authorized officer from the local authority may examine any food intended for human consumption, and may take samples for analysis or examination. If it is suspected that food is likely to cause food poisoning, its further use may be prohibited whilst a sample is being examined. Food considered unfit may be seized, and with the approval of a Justice of the Peace, may be condemned and disposed of so that it cannot be used for human consumption.

Food and Drugs (Control of Food Premises) Act 1976

This is an amendment to the *Food and Drugs Act 1955.* It prohibits the preparation, storage and sale of food in certain circumstances, e.g. where a person has been convicted of an offence under Section 13 of the *Food and Drugs Act 1955,* if the offence relates to a food business where food is exposed to the risk of contamination. A 'closure order' may be issued if it is felt that the unsatisfactory conditions are likely to continue and be a danger to health.

An 'emergency order' may be made if there is imminent risk of danger to health. This could prohibit the use of premises pending the outcome of a prosecution under the Act.

The Food Hygiene (General) Regulations 1970

These Regulations are made under the *Food and Drugs Act 1955* and aim to ensure a high standard of construction of food premises, high standards of maintenance of these premises and proper conduct by food handlers to prevent the contamination of food. The requirements are described in Volume 1. Conviction under these regulations may result in a fine of up to £100 or three months' imprisonment.

The Shops Act 1960

Despite its name, this Act does affect accommodation and cleaning services. It is illegal to employ waitresses under the age of 18 after 10.00 p.m. at night, but a waiter of the same age may be employed until midnight provided he does not have to be on duty before 11.00 a.m. the following morning.

The Fire Precautions Act 1971 – Hotels and Boarding Houses

All hotels and boarding houses are covered by this Act except those not providing sleeping accommodation for more than six persons (guests or staff), provided that this sleeping accommodation is not above the first floor or below the ground floor.

The Act requires those in charge of hotels and boarding houses to take adequate measures to deal with fire and its hazards. Adequate means of escape and fire precautions must be provided in all places of public entertainment, resorts and in certain residential establishments, e.g. old people's homes. Premises covered by the Act must obtain a Fire Certificate from the local area fire authority. A certificate is also necessary when a hotel is used to store explosive or highly flammable substances, no matter how many guests are accommodated:

The certificate will be granted after inspection and approval by the authority and will specify:

- The particular use of the premises which it covers.
- The means of escape in case of fire (a plan will often be used for this purpose).
- The precautions required by the Act relating to the means of escape, fire-resisting doors, ventilation, emergency lighting, means of giving warning in case of fire, fire-fighting equipment, fire instruction and drills, construction and layout of accommodation and furnishings, training and management of staff.

Notification of Accidents and Dangerous Occurrences 1980

The act requires all accidents and dangerous occurrences to be reported to the appropriate authority. It covers all workers. Minor incidents involving over three days' absence will be reported automatically to the Health and Safety Executive by the DHSS. Fatalities, major injuries and notifiable dangerous occurrences must be reported immediately to the enforcing authority, e.g. HSE, followed by a written report within seven days.

A fatality will include employees and members of the general public who die within one year of the accident.

A major injury includes: fracture of skull, spine and pelvis; fracture of any bone other than hand, foot, ankle or wrist; amputation of part or all of a limb, loss of an eye, any injury resulting in a person being detained in hospital for more than 24 hours (other than for general observation).

Dangerous occurrences include: collapse of lifts, hoists, scaffold; explosion or bursting of boilers; electrical faults leading to a fire or explosion; release of flammable material or other dangerous substance; collapse of all or part of a building; inhalation of dangerous substances; ill health caused by microbiological agents (pathogens).

All accidents must be entered in an accident book kept on the premises. The details required are described on page 34.

Accidents

The effective prevention of accidents depends on three things: training, hazard spotting and prevention, and procedures in the event of an accident.

Training

Training should include courses specifically concerned with safety matters and safety training should form part of any training session or course.

Hazard spotting and prevention

All members of staff have responsibilities relating to health and safety at work and maximum participation is thus desirable. If each grade of staff or each department has a specific person designated or elected as safety representative, then the organization has the basis of a safety committee which should meet regularly to discuss specific safety measures, training and development and also undertake regular safety inspections of the whole establishment. When regular safety inspections are to be carried out, the safety committee should agree a list to be checked in each department, i.e. hazard-spotting checklist (see Figure 14).

Alternatively, the checklist could be completed by the departmental head at stated intervals and then presented to the safety committee and management for consideration and any necessary action.

It is helpful to include in the team people from outside the department being checked, as they are less likely to overlook obvious faults. Even when such routine safety inspections are carried out, it is still essential for all staff employers/ees to be vigilant at all times to ensure that the occurrence of accidents is minimized.

Table 2 summarizes the main type of accident, their causes and methods of prevention.

Accident reporting

If, despite training and vigilance, accidents occur it is a legal requirement that fatalities and major injuries must be reported immediately to the relevant enforcing authority. The accident report subsequently made in writing should provide the following information:

- Personal particulars of persons injured.
- Date and time of accident.
- Where and how the accident happened.
- Nature and extent of injuries occurring.
- Particulars of any witnesses.
- Description of any treatment given and by whom.

In any organization or company an accident book must be kept on the premises. If it is not the employer's premises or his principal premises then records should also be kept at head office. The accident book must show for any accident:

- Date and time of accident.
- Personal particulars of person(s) injured.

SAFETY INSPECTION REPORT

Department Domestic Services   Date 12·6·81

Area	Item	Hazard	Effect of hazard	Immediate action	Long-term action
Staff Changing Room	Floor	cracked PVC tile	falls likely	refer to maintenance for replacement	plan for complete replacement of floor tiles.
	Walls	✓			
	Heating	✓			
	Lighting	✓			
	Extractors	✓			
	Lockers	✓			
	Seating	✓			
	Waste Bins	✓			
	Mirrors	✓			
	Changing cubicles	insecure curtain rail	head injuries	refer to maintenance for refixing	replace rails with stronger system
Machine Store	Floor	✓			

Head of Department: M Jones

Figure 14 *Hazard-spotting checklist*

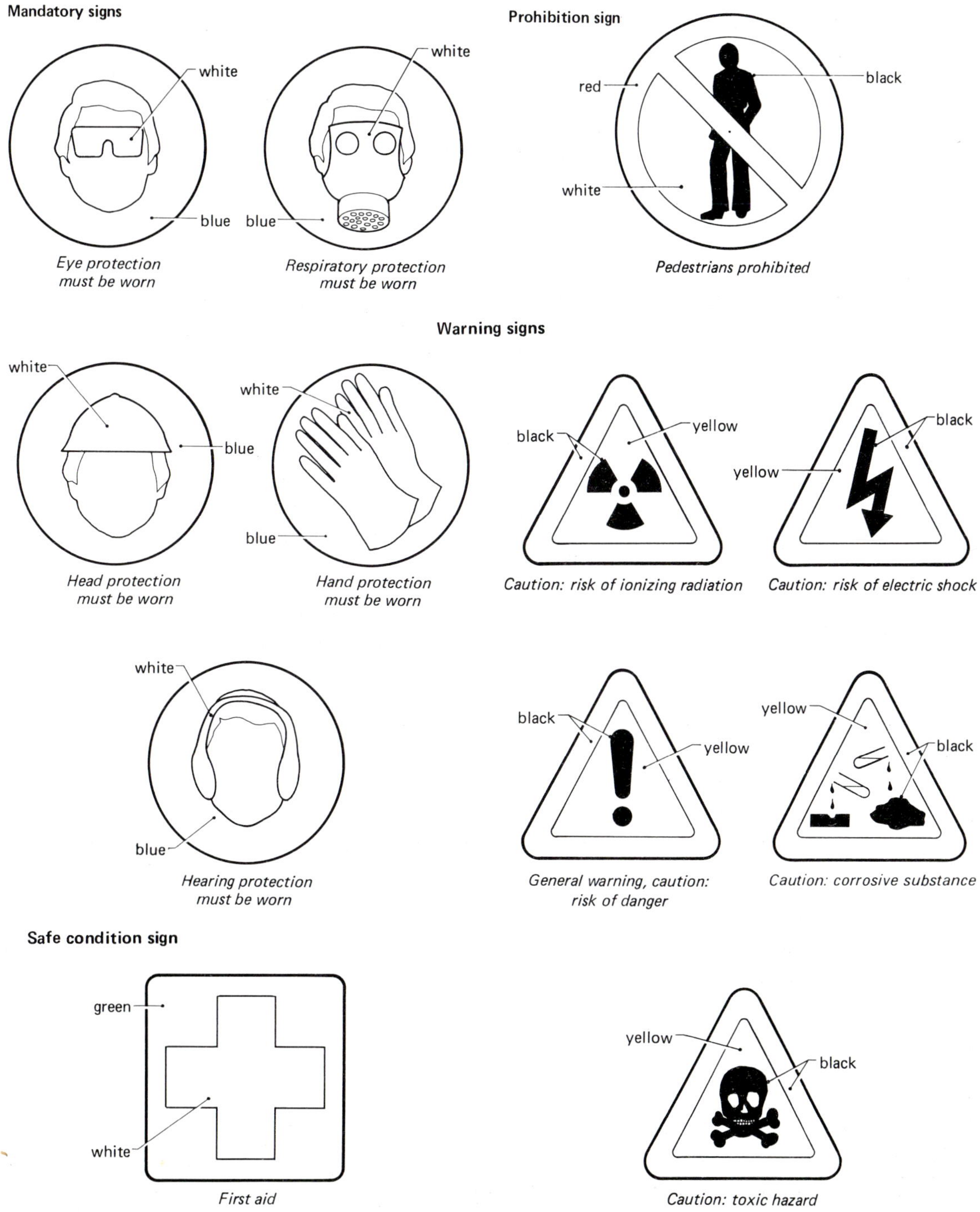
Mandatory signs
white
blue
Eye protection must be worn
white
blue
Respiratory protection must be worn
Prohibition sign
red
black
white
Pedestrians prohibited
Warning signs
white
blue
Head protection must be worn
white
blue
Hand protection must be worn
black
yellow
Caution: risk of ionizing radiation
black
yellow
Caution: risk of electric shock
white
blue
Hearing protection must be worn
black
yellow
General warning, caution: risk of danger
yellow
black
Caution: corrosive substance
Safe condition sign
green
white
First aid
yellow
black
Caution: toxic hazard

Figure 15 *Safety warning signs*

Table 2 *Common hazards and their prevention*

Type and cause	Prevention
Falls	
Objects and equipment or rubbish left in corridors or on stairs	Remove all potential hazards Use warning signs if unavoidable
Furniture out of place	Return to usual place
Electric flexes left in passage way	Position in least dangerous place Use cable tidily Place flex over shoulder Run flex over door handles Remove flex immediately after use Avoid excess lengths of flex
Spillages creating wet or greasy floors	Wipe up immediately and train staff to always observe this point Use warning signs
Poor floor maintenance procedures	Use warning signs Cordon area involved Arrange work to be carried out when traffic is minimal Always try to leave a safe, dry area for traffic Do not leave floor wet Avoid excessive use and build-up of polish
Loose carpet treads, carpets, bannisters, worn floors	Report and ensure repairs are carried out Use warning signs until repair has been completed Use cordons if necessary
Climbing on unsafe ladders	Secure ladders correctly Ensure that ladder is the correct height for the job Use warning signs Use cordons Check and maintain ladders regularly Use in accordance with locally negotiated agreements
Climbing on furniture, ledges, etc.	Never permit staff to do this
Poor footwear	Shoes should provide adequate support and protection to feet Rubber soled shoes will help to eliminate risk of falls
Poor lighting	Lighting must be adequate, illuminating the whole area and leaving no dark areas

Table 2 *continued*

Type and cause	Prevention
Rushing	Do not rush Use handrails where provided On stairs, travel one step at a time Do not read, etc., on stairs
Back strain	
Incorrect carrying, lifting, pushing	Train staff in correct methods of lifting, carrying, pushing Use specialized equipment whenever available Check and maintain trolleys and equipment regularly
Overloading of trolleys	Never overload trolleys
Lifting too heavy a weight	Never attempt to lift too heavy a weight
Cuts and bumps	
Opening doors	Approach all doors carefully Open all doors carefully Beware swing doors Always use doors marked IN and OUT correctly Glass doors should be marked or have warning signs
Overloading of trolleys, etc.	Never overload trolleys
Knives, tools	Use with care Follow correct procedure for washing or cleaning Store correctly
Handling of waste, e.g. glass	Wear gloves Ensure no sharp edges Follow specialist advice for disposal of items such as syringes
Burns, scalds, inhalation	
Hot liquids	Handle with care Never store above waist height
Handling chemicals	Ventilate in confined areas Wear protective clothing, e.g. gloves, masks, overalls Do not mix chemicals Label correctly Store correctly

(continued)

Table 2 *continued*

Type and cause	Prevention
Shock	
Bad practice	Always turn off appliance before disconnecting
	Always disconnect from mains after use or when maintaining appliance
	Do not pull on flexes
	Use correct fuses
	Do not overload power outlets
	Ensure that hands are dry and that there is no water around
	Ensure that flexes are of suitable length
Faulty appliances	Regular checking and maintenance of appliances
Falling objects	
Equipment falling from ladders, ledges, etc.	Secure all equipment
	Use warning signs
	Cordon off area
	Store all equipment correctly

- Nature of injury.
- Place of occurrence.
- Description of circumstances.
- Signature of supervisor or manager.

Investigation of accidents and analysis of reports will be essential to prevent future occurrences.

British Standards

BS 5378:1980, *Safety Signs and Colours. Part 1: Specification for colour and design*

See also standards listed after the section dealing with fire in this chapter and after the sections dealing with the various types of cleaning and access equipment in Volume 1.

First aid

Legal requirements

The *Offices, Shops and Railway Premises Act 1963*

lays down certain requirements in respect of first-aid procedures:

- A first-aid box or cupboard should be provided for the use of employees in all premises and must be readily accessible.
- Where more than 150 persons are employed at one time, an additional box or cupboard must be provided for every additional 150 persons or fraction of that number.
- Each first-aid box or cupboard must be placed in the charge of a responsible person and no person may be in charge of more than one box or cupboard.
- The first-aid box or cupboard must contain only first-aid requisites and must include those prescribed by the *Offices, Shops and Railway Premises First Aid Order 1964*. These include: sterilized unmedicated dressings; adhesive wound dressings; triangular bandages; adhesive plaster; cotton wool; sterilized eye pads; safety pins; rubber or

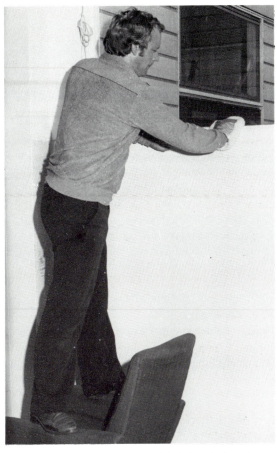

Unsafe (left) and safe (right) high-level cleaning

pressure bandage (except in offices and shops where not more than ten persons are employed).

First-aid methods

In addition to complying with these legal requirements, it is advantageous for all staff employed in the supervisory grades to be trained in simple first-aid techniques appropriate to accommodation services and cleaning. The methods of first aid used in the event of various types of accident include the following.

Bleeding:
1 Press edges of wound together for a few minutes.
2 Place a pad over wound.
3 Bandage.
4 If necessary place on more pads and bandage again – DO NOT remove earlier pads or bandages.
5 Place limb in raised position.
6 Do not use a tourniquet.
7 Do not remove foreign bodies unless just on surface of injury.

Nose bleed:
1 Sit subject upright with head held slightly forward.
2 Pinch lower part of nose.

Scalds and burns:
1 Smother flames if burning.

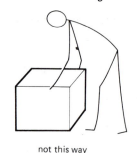

not this way

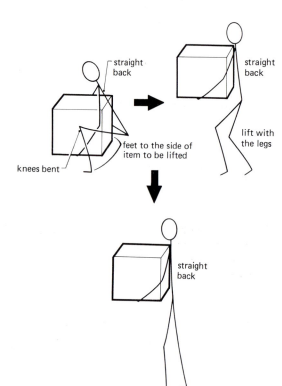

straight back

straight back

lift with the legs

feet to the side of item to be lifted

knees bent

straight back

Figure 16 *Correct method of lifting*

2 Cool area with cold water.
3 Wrap in clean sheet, etc., and take subject to hospital.
4 Do not use ointments, etc.
5 Do not try to remove clothing adhering to burns.

Shock:
1 Keep subject warm.

2 Provide small, cool drinks.
3 Do not give hot drinks.

Electric shock:
1 Switch off supply and disconnect appliance. If this is impossible stand on dry insulating material.
2 Remove subject.
3 Apply artificial respiration and heart massage as required (see below).
4 Now treat as for shock.
5 Seek medical aid.

Broken or dislocated bones:
1 Do not move subject unless unavoidable.
2 Immobilize injured part with splints, bandages or slings as appropriate.
3 Do not try to correct deformity.

Poison or drugs:
If non-corrosive cause subject to vomit by:

1 Tickling back of the throat; or
2 Making subject drink salt water.

If corrosive:

1 Give water to dilute poison.
2 Seek urgent help.
3 Do not make subject vomit.

Unconcious:
1 Place subject in the coma position (see Figure 17).
2 Give artificial respiration if necessary.

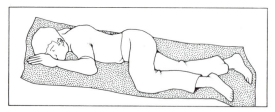

Figure 17 *Coma position*

Artificial respiration (see Figure 18):
1 Place subject on back.
2 Remove clothing from around neck.
3 Check mouth and throat for objects.

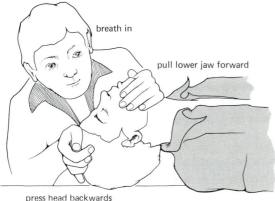

breath in

pull lower jaw forward

press head backwards

lay victim on his back and loosen clothing around neck

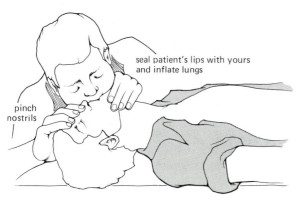

seal patient's lips with yours and inflate lungs

pinch nostrils

blow into lungs (twelve times every minute)
avoid patient's exhaled air

Figure 18 *Artificial respiration*

4 Tilt head back to open air passages.
5 Take deep breath.
6 Place mouth over subject's mouth. Pinch subject's nose. Blow out gently. Note that chest rises.
7 Remove mouth and allow chest to fall naturally.
8 Repeat steps 5, 6 and 7 every 4–5 seconds until natural breathing starts.

Heart has stopped:

Heart massage/cardiac compression may be administered, but only by a trained first-aider. Great damage can be done if this method is incorrectly applied. Only administer if heart has stopped, i.e. no pulse, pupils dilated.

1 Strike breast bone sharply with hand once or twice. If heart does not start, then commence massage.
2 Inflate subject's lungs as for 'artificial respiration'.
3 Place heel of hand over breast bone where ribs meet.
4 Place other hand on top of first.
5 Press firmly on lower half of breast bone and repeat every 4–5 seconds.
6 Repeat 2 to 5 indefinitely until help arrives.

Choking:

1 Remove object from throat or mouth taking great care.
2 Grasp subject from behind with one arm across subject's chest, below rib cage.
3 Grasp first hand with other and jerk to expel air and hence the object.
4 If this fails take the subject to hospital as quickly as possible.

Concussion:

1 Place in coma position – avoids danger of choking if subject vomits.
2 Keep warm.
3 Seek medical aid.

Drowning:

1 Turn subject upside down to drain lungs.
2 Give artificial respiration and heart massage as necessary.
3 Get medical aid.

Suffocation:

1 Remove cause of suffocation.
2 Treat as for drowning.

It must be emphasized that training and updating of first-aid procedures is essential if the administration of first aid is to be effective at all times.

Fire

It is essential that all staff should be made aware of the causes of fires and their prevention and are trained in their firm's emergency fire drill and the

Table 3 *Causes of fire*

Cause	Prevention
Smoking and matches	1 No smoking allowed in restricted or unattended areas 2 Ash trays should be provided and emptied regularly 3 All cigarette ends must be extinguished 4 No smoking allowed in chemical stores
Electrical	1 Regular checking and maintenance of electrical appliances, flexes, plugs, etc. 2 Regular checking of wiring of building. Renew when necessary 3 Train staff never to use faulty appliances 4 Do not permit overloading of power outlets
Heating equipment	1 Use fire guards 2 Position fires away from furnishings 3 Ensure that the size of heating appliance is appropriate to size of the room
Spontaneous combustion	1 Cloths should be disposed of correctly, particularly polish cloths 2 Take care when dealing with soiled wet mattresses 3 Waste materials must be covered and stored correctly 4 Aerosols must not be heated or burnt
Storage of chemicals	1 All chemicals, e.g. cleaning agents with low flash points (meths, turps, polish, etc.), must be stored in a special store 2 Inflammable liquids, e.g. chemical solvents, must be kept away from naked lights

correct use of fire extinguishers and appliances.

Causes and prevention

Some of the main causes of fire and their prevention are shown in Table 3.

Procedure in the event of a fire

Staff training should be systematic and on-going. It should include:

1 The procedure in the event of a fire.
2 The location of exits and escape routes and that they must never be locked or blocked.

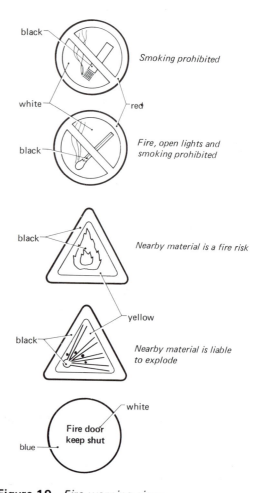

Figure 19 *Fire warning signs*

3 The location of fire extinguishers and their use.

In rooms occupied by guests or residents there must be a notice indicating:

a   Location of nearest exit.
b   The escape route.
c   Action in event of fire.

Procedure in the event of a fire must be:

1 Activate alarm.
2 Inform switchboard/call fire brigade.
3 Vacate building using appropriate route. Close all doors and windows on leaving. Do not panic. Do not use lifts (if in one, get out at next floor and switch off).
4 Tackle fire if no personal risk involved.
5 Assemble outside building and carry out roll call if appropriate

Fire precautions

A number of measures can be taken to prevent and contain fires and to reduce the hazards involved in the event of a fire. All must be tested periodically.

Sprinklers A system of pipes built into the ceilings and connected to the mains water supply. At intervals sprinklers (openings) are situated which open when the temperature rises to a pre-determined level.

Automatic alarms Detectors situated in the ceiling of each room or corridor of a building. They are sensitive to smoke or heat and in the event of a fire activate the alarm.

Manual alarms Situated at various intervals throughout a building. They are set off by the individual finding a fire. The alarm will be linked to a central indicator which will show the location of the fire. It may also be linked to the local fire brigade.

Fire escape routes A safe means of escape will be required from each floor and part of a building.

Fire escape door complete with notices and crash bar

They will frequently involve the installation of fire escapes and escape doors. Escape doors must never be locked but where locking is necessary a key must be provided. Panic bolts where doors are opened in this way must work. Exit routes must be sign-posted and must never be blocked.

Fire doors Fitted to rooms and at intervals along corridors. Depending on the room and situation these doors will have a half-hour, e.g. bedrooms, and one-hour rating. They must always work. Manually closing doors must never be jammed open. Doors may also be self-closing.

Escape drills A procedure in the event of a fire

must exist. It should be known by all staff and be tested regularly.

Emergency lighting must be provided on an independent circuit so that emergency exit routes and signs are illuminated even if main circuit fails. It will operate automatically.

Fire extinguishers

Fires require fuel and oxygen (see Figure 20). Fire-fighting appliances either exclude oxygen from the fire or cool the combustible material to below its ignition temperature. The ignition temperature is the temperature below which a combustible material will not burn.

When dealing with a fire it is essential that the correct appliance is used. Selection of the wrong appliance can accelerate the spread of the fire rather than control it. Table 4 and Figure 21 give the main types of fire extinguisher, their uses and methods of use. In buildings over five storeys there should also be rising mains, i.e. pipes to which firemen fit their hoses.

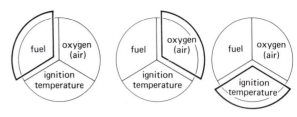

Remove either the fuel or the oxygen or cool the fire below its ignition temperature and the fire will be extinguished.

Figure 20   *Basic needs of a fire*

British Standards

BS 5306:1980, *Code of Practice for Fire Extinguishing Installations and Equipment on Premises. Part 3: Portable fire extinguishers*

BS 5423:1977, *Specification for Portable Fire Extinguishers.*

BS 5499:1978, *Fire Safety Signs, Notices and Graphic Symbols. Part 1: Specification for fire safety signs.*

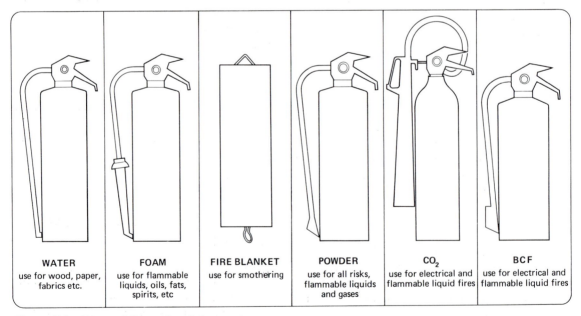

WATER	FOAM	FIRE BLANKET	POWDER	CO$_2$	BCF
use for wood, paper, fabrics etc.	use for flammable liquids, oils, fats, spirits, etc	use for smothering	use for all risks, flammable liquids and gases	use for electrical and flammable liquid fires	use for electrical and flammable liquid fires

Figure 21   *Types of fire extinguisher*

Table 4 *Fire extinguishers*

Type	Uses	Method	Never use
Fire hose	General fires, e.g. wood, paper, textiles or similar, requiring quenching or cooling	Connect to mains water supply. Direct at base of fire and systematically cover the combustible material	Electrical or liquid fires
Water-filled	As fire hose	Direct at base of fire and systematically cover the combustible material	Electrical or liquid fires
Carbon dioxide and dry powder	Burning liquids and electrical fires	Direct at the base of electrical fires. For burning liquids spread contents by a sweeping action, systematically covering the fire until flames engulfed	
BCF	As carbon dioxide and dry powder	As carbon dioxide and dry powder	Not suitable in confined spaces. Dangerous fumes produced
Foam: A small canister within a large one, containing chemicals which when mixed form a foam	Burning liquids	Apply a layer of foam systematically over the fire starting from the back	
Fire blanket	Burning liquids	Cover fire	

Note 1 Used appliances must be refilled or replaced immediately after use
Note 2 Regular checking and maintenance of appliances is essential

Welfare

Although the *Health and Safety at Work etc. Act 1974* obliges employers to take care of the welfare of all staff, it does not actually define this term. One possible definition could be the 'demonstration of concern for the human needs of staff'.

This could take into account the provision of suitable facilities for:

- Meals.
- Accommodation, e.g. rest-room, dining room, cloakrooms, residences.
- Amenities, e.g. sports and social facilities.

- Appreciation of the needs of different age groups, e.g. acting *in loco parentis* to young staff.

Welfare of staff should also include evidence of concern for staff, both as individuals and as part of a team. The attitude of the supervisor is of great importance here, since most staff prefer to regard their supervisor as someone to whom they can take worries and problems, knowing that they will receive a fair and sympathetic hearing, and direction in gaining specialist advice if necessary.

4 Work study

Work study provides a way of systematically examining a problem or area of work in order to develop objective alternatives for the solution of particular problems. It is normally carried out by a specialist in the field of work study, who is employed to carry out the work on a full-time basis and who is not part of the workforce involved in the area of study. It is important, however, that all staff involved in work organization and planning should have a general knowledge of the techniques used in work study and be able to employ its principles.

Principles of work study

Work study (see Figure 22) involves two branches, method study and work measurement, which can be employed to increase productivity in the work place. The main benefits of work study are:

- Work place layout improved.
- Equipment design improved.
- Working environment improved.
- Planning and control improved.
- Staff levels correctly determined.
- Better control data made available.
- Health and safety of visitors, staff, residents, etc. improved.

These will result in:

1 Reduction in fatigue.
2 More cost-effective use of manpower, materials and equipment.

Work study also provides a sound basis for the introduction of incentive schemes.

Stages involved in a complete work study

1 The work to be studied is *selected*.

2 The work is observed and these observations are *recorded* in the most suitable manner, so that there is a bank of relevant information available for analysis.
3 The recorded facts are *examined* critically and every stage of the work is questioned and challenged.
4 The most efficient method within the given constraints is *developed*.
5 The new method is *measured* so that a standard time for its completion may be calculated.
6 The new, timed method is *defined* for ease of identification.
7 The new method and its time standard/allowed time is *installed*.
8 The new method and time standard/allowed time is controlled and *maintained*.

It is essential that both management and management services staff recognize the need for the establishment of good relationships with all staff involved in any way with an area of work to be studied, as most staff will fear the unknown and will find that the introduction of work study is

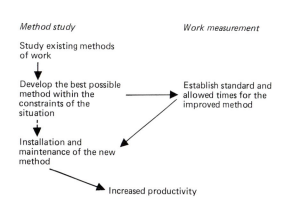

Figure 22 *Outline of work study*

stressful. The establishment and maintenance of good channels of communication and regular explanation and consultation with staff will help to overcome some of these problems. The attitude of both management and management services staff will be very important.

Method study

Method study is defined as the 'systematic recording and critical examination of existing and proposed ways of doing work, as a means of developing and applying easier and more effective methods and reducing costs'. The aims of method study are to:

1   Improve processes, procedures and methods of work.
2   Improve the layout of the workplace.
3   Improve the design of equipment and plant.
4   Improve the use of resources.
5   Improve the working environment.
6   Reduce unnecessary fatigue by reducing human effort.

Although there are various techniques used in method study, the basic procedure to be followed is the same.

Selection of the work to be studied (1)

Some indications that method study is required may be:

1   Labour-intensive work, particularly highly repetitive work.
2   'Bottlenecks' which delay other areas of work.
3   High labour turnover.
4   High accident rate.
5   Frequent unsatisfactory work.
6   Inability to complete work within allocated time.
7   Non-emergency overtime.
8   Consumer complaints.

It is also important to consider the economic importance of the work to be studied, the availability of adequate technical knowledge of the area of work and the likely human reactions to work study. Even if the proposed area of study is of major economic importance, if the study will lead to unrest or ill-feeling amongst employees in that area of work, it may be better to postpone one study and try to gain employee confidence by studying other areas, e.g. unpopular tasks, where the benefits to the workforce may be easily seen, before returning to the originally proposed area of study.

The areas of work to be studied will often be selected by management or, occasionally, may be requested by trade unions. However, in most cases the main factor to be taken into consideration will be the economic one, i.e. the expected savings brought about by method study must be balanced against the cost of carrying out the study and its implementation. Recent legislation, particularly the *Health and Safety at Work etc. Act 1974* and changes in laws relating to product liability, will also indicate those areas of work to be studied.

Definition of the problem (2)

As with any method of problem-solving, in work study the definition of the problem is of vital importance, and so, each potential area of study should be assessed. It is necessary to have full background details available. For example:

How much work is accomplished at each stage?
How long will the work exist and will there be any variations in the work?
How many staff are engaged in this work directly or indirectly?
What are the grades and rates of pay of these staff?
What is the average output per member or team of staff per day?
How is payment made?
What is the potential output per member or team of staff per day?
What equipment is available and what is its cost?
Is the work place layout satisfactory?
What is the quality of the work required?
How is the quality of work controlled?

Table 5 *Commonly used symbols*

Symbol	Name	Definition
◯	Operation	The main stages in a method or procedure, during which the material or product is modified or changed
▢	Inspection	A check or inspection for quality and/or quantity. The material or product is not changed
▷	Transport	The movement of operatives, materials, goods or equipment. This symbol represents movement from place to place, but not those movements which naturally occur within an operation or inspection
D	Delay or temporary storage	A delay in the sequence of events or the temporary setting aside of an object without record until required e.g. letter waiting to be signed
▽	Permanent storage	Materials are issued or received into storage with some form of authorization, e.g. requisition
▣	Combined activities	Where activities occur simultaneously the symbols of the activities are combined

Can savings or improvements be made in the methods employed?

With this background information plus valid reasons for the need for a method study investigation, it should be possible to assess the value of the study.

Recording of the facts (3)

Having defined the problem, all facts relevant to the area of work being studied must be recorded. Traditionally, facts are recorded by the written word, however, this method of recording is inefficient and unsuitable when recording the complicated processes of work. The facts, therefore, are compiled into charts and diagrams using appropriate symbols (see Table 5).

Method study charts and diagrams

There are many types of charts and diagrams used in method study (see Table 6). Some of these charts and diagrams are described on the following pages.

Table 6 *Method study charts and diagrams*

Sequence	Movement	Time scale
Outline process chart	Flow diagram	Multiple activity chart
Flow process chart:	String diagram	Simo chart
man-type	Cyclegraph	PMTS chart
material-type	Chronocyclo-graph	
equipment-type	Travel chart	
Two handed process chart		

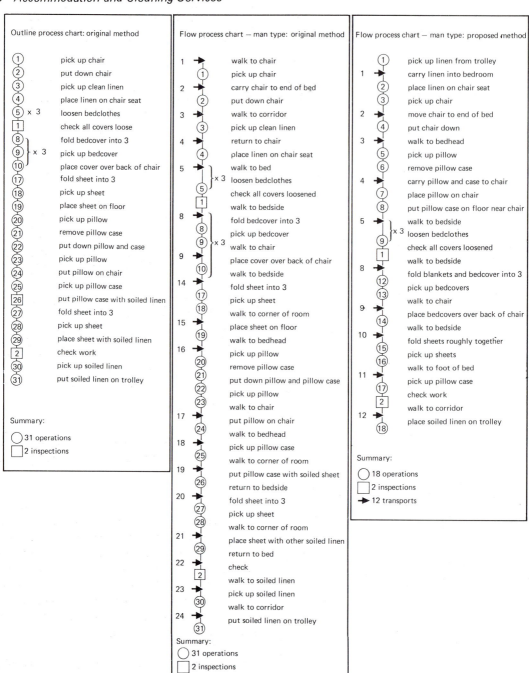

Figure 23 *Outline and flow process charts*

The outline process chart (see Figure 23) gives an overall picture by recording only the main operations and inspections. Therefore, the only symbols used are ○ and □. A brief note is made of each step in the sequence alongside each symbol. If the time taken to accomplish each step is known, it is also recorded.

The flow process chart (see Figure 23) uses all the five symbols and records the sequence of the flow of the procedure or product. The three types of flow process chart are:

1 Man-type, which records what the operative does.
2 Material-type, which records what is happening to the material.
3 Equipment-type, which records how the equipment is being used.

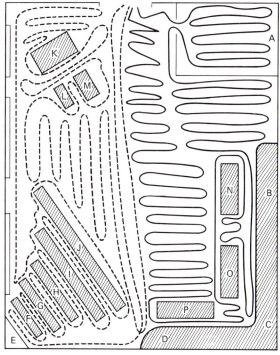

Dust Control Mopping : domestic assistant A ———
domestic assistant B - - - - - -

Figure 25 *String diagram*

When flow process charts are being used frequently it is convenient to use pre-printed forms.

The flow diagram (see Figure 24) is used to supplement the flow process chart. It is a scale plan of the workplace on to which the movement of materials or products can be recorded. The process chart symbols may be added to show the activities carried out in each area of the workplace. A flow diagram may be three-dimensional, where the movement of materials is carried out on different floors of a building.

The string diagram (see Figure 25) consists of a scale plan or model on which a thread or string is used to record and measure the path taken by operatives, materials or equipment within the area of study. It is often used to supplement a flow process chart to provide a clear picture of what is

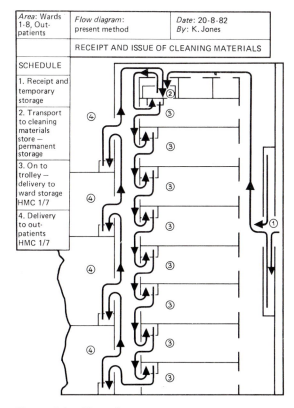

Figure 24 *Flow diagram*

being done. It is most frequently used to show the movements of operatives, and should not be used where a flow diagram would suffice since it is complicated to prepare.

The travel chart Where patterns of movement are complex, the travel chart (see Figure 26) is a quick, simple method to use. It appears as a table which shows the number of movements of operatives, materials or equipment between any number of places over a given period of time.

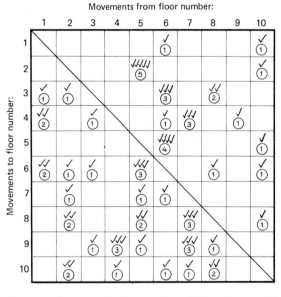

Figure 26 *Travel chart*

The travel chart is always a square, divided into smaller squares each of which represents a work station or department. The squares running horizontally from left to right represent the areas from where movement takes place, whilst those running vertically down the left-hand side show the areas to which movement is made. Journeys are recorded with a mark, e.g. a tick in the square of the department of arrival.

Time	Original method		Proposed method	
	Operative A	Operative B	Operative A	Operative B
9.00	Collect equipment and materials	Collect equipment and materials	Collect equipment and materials	Collect equipment and materials
	Remove litter Dust control mop	Remove litter Dust control mop	Assemble scrubber polisher	Put out warning signs
	Put out warning signs	Put out warning signs		Dust control mop half floor
	Assemble scrubber polisher	Assemble wet suction machine		Dust control mop half floor
9.30	Scrub half floor		Scrub half floor	Assemble wet suction machine
			Scrub half floor	Suction dry half floor
9.45	Scrub half floor	Suction dry half floor		Suction dry half floor
			Empty tank and fill with water	Suction dry half floor
10.00	Empty tank and fill with water	Suction dry half floor	Scrub rinse half floor	
	Scrub rinse half floor			
			Scrub rinse half floor	Suction dry half floor
10.15	Scrub rinse half floor	Suction dry half floor	Scrub rinse half floor	Suction dry half floor
			Empty and clean scrubber polisher	Empty and clean wet suction machine
10.30	Empty and clean scrubber polisher	Suction dry half floor	Put equipment away	Collect signs
	Collect signs	Empty and clean wet suction machine		Put signs equipment away
10.45	Put equipment away	Put equipment away		

Key  working time / ineffective time

Figure 27 *Multiple activity chart*

The multiple activity chart (see Figure 27) is a chart upon which the activities of more than one subject, i.e. operative, machine or equipment, are recorded on a common time scale and is used to show their relationship.

The chart is drawn up using a vertical column or bar to represent the activities of each subject, alongside a time scale, so that periods of idleness can be clearly seen. The study of a well constructed chart may show ways in which activities can be rearranged so that ineffective time can be reduced. It is extremely useful when organizing team-work or maintenance work and when determining the number of machines or processes one employee can look after.

Examination of the recorded facts (4)

Once the activities under study have been recorded, the information must be critically examined using a questioning technique whereby each activity is systematically subjected in turn to a progressive series of questions.

The questioning technique is designed to eliminate, combine, rearrange or simplify the recorded activities. There are two stages in the questioning technique, primary and secondary – see Table 7. The aim of the primary questions is to eliminate as many non-productive or unnecessary activities as possible, therefore enabling the use of the secondary questions to lead to the production of alternatives which will achieve a better method.

Development of the improved method (5)

The development of the most appropriate improved method can only be achieved by the systematic use of the questioning technique. Alternative methods are developed which should be charted so that they may be compared with the original method. In this way it will be possible to summarize the savings in time and distance which may be expected from the introduction of a particular method. (At this stage it may be

Table 7

Question	Primary	Aim	Secondary
Purpose	What is achieved? Why is the activity necessary?	To eliminate unnecessary stages of work.	What else could be done? What should be done?
Place	Where is it done? Why is it done there?		Where else could it be done? Where should it be done?
Sequence	When is it done? Why is it done then?	To combine where possible or to rearrange the sequence of activities for more effective results.	When could it be done? When should it be done?
Person	Who is doing it? Why is it done by that person?		Who else could do it? Who should do it?
Means	How is it being done? Why is it being done that way?	To simplify the operation.	How else could it be done? How should it be done?

necessary to use work measurement techniques to measure savings in time.)

Once the various alternatives have been developed and the possible improvements determined, the development of the new method can be completed and introduced.

Definition of the improved method (6)

Once the improved method has been developed, approval should be obtained for its installation. A concise report should be prepared comparing the existing and the proposed new method. It should include the expected savings in labour, materials and overheads, the cost of implementation of the new method and management action necessary for the implementation of the new method.

A simplified outline of the main contents and the format of a report based on the multiple activity chart, Figure 27, might be as follows.

1 The objective of the study To balance the work load of the floor maintenance team and reduce ineffective time.

2 The existing and proposed methods Details of the two methods are described together with any supporting diagrams or charts.

3 The justification for the proposal
 3.1 Reduction in labour costs
 Reduction in time for
 Operative A using proposed
 method   8 min
 Reduction in time for
 Operative B using proposed
 method   8 min

 Total reduction in time using ———
 proposed method   16 min

The same procedure is normally carried out by four floor teams, and it is carried out by each team 10 times per week, 52 weeks per annum.

The expected total reduction in time per annum will be (16 min × 52 weeks × 10 × 4 teams):   555 hr

Labour costs are currently £2 per hour.
The expected total reduction in labour costs will be (£2 × 555 hr):   £1,110

The reduction in time may be allocated to additional work or lead eventually to a reduction in staff.

3.2 Balancing of work load

	Operative A	Operative B
Original method, min	100	58
Proposed method, min	92	70

Although the work loads are still unequal it is recommended that operatives reverse roles on alternate days.

4 Installation of the new method This would involve staff training, rescheduling and re-allocation of work.

Once the new method has been approved, it must be carefully defined. This definition may take the form of a written standard practice or 'operator instruction sheet' which outlines the method to be used by the operative, the tools and equipment to be used, the general operating conditions and a diagram of the workplace layout with sketches of special tools if appropriate. This document has several functions:

1 It records the new method for future reference.
2 It helps to explain the new methods to all groups of staff involved.
3 It helps to advise other departments, e.g. maintenance engineers of any new equipment or maintenance required.
4 It assists with the training of new staff or the retraining of existing staff.

5 It can form the basis for work measurement for the setting of time standards.

Installation of the new method (7)

The new method will be installed once acceptance, support and cooperation by both management and trade unions or staff representatives is achieved. This can be the most difficult part of the whole method study process as it depends to a large extent on the ability of the work study officer to communicate his ideas clearly and simply and his ability to gain the trust of all staff involved in his new scheme.

The stages of installation are:

1 Acceptance of the new method by departmental supervisor or manager.
2 Acceptance of the new method by general management.
3 Acceptance of the new method by staff and their representatives.
4 Retraining of staff to operate the new methods.
5 Monitoring the progress of the work until the new method is running smoothly.

Maintenance of the new method (8)

Once the new method has been installed and is running smoothly it is important that it be maintained and that employees are not allowed to return to old methods. Such maintenance can only be achieved where the new method has been precisely documented, where staff have received sufficient training and where there is efficient supervision and control of standards.

Work measurement

The second branch of work study, work measurement, involves the measurement of human effort and is concerned with the investigation, reduction and elimination of ineffective time, i.e. time during which no useful work is being carried out. As its name implies, work measurement deals with measuring the time taken to complete tasks or sections of tasks so that

ineffective and effective time may be separated. It can also be used to set time standards for carrying out operations with which the actual time taken to carry out those operations may be compared so that deviation from the time standard can be highlighted and corrected.

Work measurement techniques should follow method study to ensure that the time standards being established relate to the most efficient method of carrying out the work. They may be used to:

● Form the basis of time/cost control.
● Form the basis of budgetary control.
● Provide the essential information for the preparation of price estimates, delivery dates and tenders.
● Form the basis for production planning and control.
● Compare the efficiency of alternative method of work.
● Balance the work load of members of a team.
● Provide the basis for the preparation of financial incentive bonus schemes.
● Determine the number of machines which one person can operate.

The stages involved in work measurement are:

1 *Selection* of the work to be studied.
2 *Recording* of all information relevant to the circumstances in which the work is being carried out, the methods used and the elements of activity within them.
3 *Critical examination* of the recorded information to ensure that the most effective methods are being used and that productive and unproductive elements of the work can be separated.
4 *Measurement* in time of the quantity of work in each element.
5 *Calculation* of the standard time for the completion of the work which will include allowances to cover relaxation, personal needs, contingencies, etc.
6 *Precise definition* of the series of tasks and the methods of work for which the standard time has been compiled. The time standard for this work can then be determined and issued.

These stages will only be necessary when the aim of work measurement is to achieve a standard time for a job. If work measurement is only being used to highlight ineffective time or to compare alternative methods, as part of method study, only steps 1 to 4 are likely to be needed.

A range of techniques can be used in work measurement. These include: time study; synthesis; predetermined motion time study; activity sampling; estimating; analytical estimating; comparative estimating. Of these techniques, time study and synthesis will be briefly described.

Time study

Time study is a work measurement technique for recording the times and rates of working for the elements of a specified job carried out under specified conditions and for analysing the data so as to obtain the time necessary for carrying out the job at a defined level of performance.

Time study equipment   The equipment used when carrying out a time study includes a stopwatch, a study/clip boad, pencils, preprinted time study forms, a reliable clock with a seconds hand, a calculating machine, a slide-rule and measuring equipment, e.g. tape measure, micrometer, steel rule, pedometer.

Stages involved in making a time study   The stages are as follows:

1   Having selected the work to be measured, ensure that the personnel to be observed are 'qualified workers', i.e. staff ' who have the necessary physical attributes, who possess the required intelligence and education, and who have acquired the necessary skill and knowledge to carry out the work to satisfactory standards of safety, quantity and quality'.
2   Observe and record all information available about the job, the operative and any surrounding conditions likely to affect the work.

3   Break down the work into recognizable 'elements' and record a complete description of the work.
4   Check that the most efficient methods of work are being used.
5   Measure the time taken by the operative to carry out each 'element' of work.
6   Simultaneously, rate or assess the effective speed of the work in relation to a concept of the standard rate or speed of the work.
7   Produce basic times, i.e. 'the time for carrying out an element of work at standard rating' for each element recorded.
8   Calculate the average basic time for each element.
9   Calculate and add the percentage allowances to be made for personal needs, relaxation, contingencies to the average basic time for each element to give the standard time.
10 Calculate the standard time for the complete job, by adding the standard time for each element and by taking into account the frequencies with which each element occurs.

Synthesis

'A work measurement technique for building up the time for a job or parts of a job at a defined level of performance by totalling element times obtained previously from time studies on other jobs containing the elements concerned or from synthetic data'.

Synthesis is used as a substitute for an individual time study where the elements of a job have been studied many times previously so that accurate representative times for them may be compiled. Tables containing these times are known as synthetic data.

The main reasons for the increasing use of synthesis are that it eliminates the need for lengthy, expensive time studies and produces a representative time based on a larger number of observations than would be practicable when using time study.

The use of synthetic data and the calculation of standard times and time standards/allowed times for a job are described in Chapter 5.

Financial incentives

Financial incentive schemes based on the techniques of work study have been introduced into some sectors of the accommodation/cleaning services industry with the aim of increasing productivity whilst reducing costs. This aim should be achieved by improving:

1 Methods of work.
2 Attitudes towards organizational goals/objectives.
3 The average rate of working and the effectiveness of employees.
4 Cooperation.

There are many types of incentive scheme available, all of which may achieve these results in varying degrees. Whichever type of scheme is to be introduced, the main requirements are that:

a It should foster complete trust between employer and employee, and so must be fair to both sides.
b It should be easy to understand.
c Employees should be able to calculate and check their wages without difficulty.
d There should be an obvious, direct relationship between effort and financial reward.

Schemes where the individual employee is paid in proportion to his efforts are usually more effective, and so should be introduced whenever possible in preference to group schemes. Where it is only practicable to introduce a scheme that is based on a group of employees, it should be confined to the smallest possible group, whose work should be interrelated. Bonus payments should be paid as quickly as possible. The incentive effect may be lost if variations in performance are not reflected almost immediately in the pay packet.

Steps must be taken to ensure that quality is maintained.

In order to maintain confidence and co-operation in the scheme, the work content must be measured accurately.

The scheme must protect the health, safety and welfare of employees.

Systems of incentive bonus schemes

There are four main systems of incentive bonus schemes:

1 *Straight proportional schemes* Employees' earnings vary in the same proportion as output.
2 *Regressive schemes* Employees' earnings vary proportionally less than output.
3 *Progressive schemes* Employees' earnings vary proportionally more than output.
4 *Variable schemes* Employees' earnings vary in proportions that differ at different levels of output.

The majority of schemes employed in British industry are of the straight proportional kind. Those schemes most often applied to domestic cleaning services are straight proportional schemes based on the *standard hour system*. In this system, a time value is set for each unit of output, so that the employee is paid his basic rate for achieving that unit in the permitted time, but is paid a bonus if he achieves that work in less than that time. In most domestic schemes, in order to receive a bonus, the employee must perform additional specified duties in the time saved from the initial task. The bonus payment is related proportionally to the number and quality of additional tasks completed. Many of these schemes are based on groups of staff working on the same area of the building. A simplified example of this could be as shown in Table 8.

Problems associated with the use of incentive bonus schemes

Many arguments are produced against the use of incentive bonus schemes. Some examples frequently encountered are:

1 Schemes result in increased pressure on supervisors.
2 Administrative costs outweigh savings in production costs.
3 The quality of the work will suffer.
4 Many schemes are so complicated that staff

Table 8

Time, min	Unit of output	Rate of pay	Time, min	Additional work	Actual pay
60	Spray buff areas A & B	£1.50	60	–	£1.50
60	Spray buff areas A & B	£1.50	55	–	£1.50
60	Spray buff areas A & B	£1.50	50	Wash two bed frames	£1.75

cannot understand them, and so, are of little incentive value and lead to disputes.

5 Wage drift is inevitable with incentive schemes, as output levels are controlled by agreement between employees.

6 Schemes draw attention to the pursuit of financial rather than other types of reward from work and thus may cause conflict with employees' traditional values.

None of these arguments is necessarily correct; an accurately produced scheme, coupled with good communication and consultation should prevent these problems, provided that when schemes are introduced, managers take care to allow sufficient time for staff to overcome their normal resistance to change and to train to achieve the new levels of performance. There will inevitably be some 'teething troubles' when the new scheme comes into effect; frequent monitoring will therefore be required to help deal with problems as they arise. Once the scheme has been fully implemented regular formal reviews should be carried out so that problem areas or areas of conflict can be highlighted and improved.

Ergonomics

Ergonomics is a relatively new branch of work study which aims to make the job and its environment suit the employee rather than forcing the employee to adapt himself to cope with the conditions of the job. It is an area of study that aims to maintain high productivity without undue fatigue or discomfort to employees. It covers the following aspects.

Sight and lighting

The lighting must provide sufficient, comfortable illumination for the type of work being done. Since most faculties deteriorate with age, lighting must cater for all age groups.

Colour

The selection of colour around the workplace is important psychologically and may effect the pace of work. Colour coding of related equipment and materials is helpful and may improve productivity whilst helping to eliminate mistakes, e.g. colour-coded cleaning cloths, mops, buckets, cleaning-agent dispensers, etc., for infectious areas.

Heating and ventilation

Current legislation must be taken into account here as well as general environmental hygiene.

Sound

Noise may be described as unwanted sound. Too much noise damages the hearing, upsets communication and causes loss of efficiency and concentration. High-pitched noises can be very distressing.

Seating

This should be designed to provide comfortable, necessary support, whilst allowing for variation in posture. It is essential to balance the height of seats and work benches/tables, etc.

Tools and equipment

These should be designed so that they can be used without discomfort to the human frame, e.g. correct height, hand grips.

Amenities

Cloakroom, rest-room, first aid, toilet facilities and other staff amenities should be provided.

Hygiene

Hygienic conditions in places of work should be observed at all times.

5 Planning, costing and control

The supervisor or manager of accommodation and cleaning services must be concerned with the effective utilization of resources to achieve the required standard of service. This can be achieved by conscientious planning, costing and control.

The interrelated facets of planning, costing and control are illustrated in Figure 28.

Maintenance

Preventive maintenance

Maintenance of the assets of any organization is vital if they are to be utilized most effectively. The assets with which we are concerned are:

- The interior and exterior fabric of a building.
- The furnishings and fittings of the buildings.
- Any plant and equipment used for the activities carried out in the building and for its maintenance.

It is important that any maintenance be planned and be part of a policy to ensure the efficient use of any assets, rather than carried out haphazardly or only when an emergency occurs. This will usually mean preventive maintenance, i.e. maintenance designed to keep all items in working order and prevent breakdowns.

Objectives of a maintenance programme

Before the planning of a maintenance programme can commence, the aim of the programme must be established. The ideal would be to maintain assets in their original state, i.e. as purchased. However, because of the constraints of time, expense and the need for availability of each item, this will usually be impossible. Most organizations will plan maintenance to achieve one or both of the following objectives.

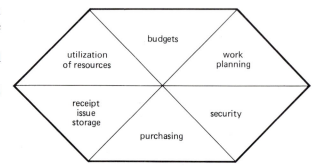

Figure 28 *Facets of planning, costing and control*

Planned deterioration An item of equipment may have an average lifespan of seven years if satisfactorily maintained, at the end of which it will be useless. The maintenance programme will be planned to provide the amount of maintenance necessary to control deterioration and keep the equipment operating as efficiently as possible for seven years. The programme would also plan for a replacement item of equipment to be purchased before the first item deteriorates completely.

Purchase and disposal of short-life products Items of equipment of low capital cost designed to be of limited life span and deemed 'short-life' items will be used with the minimum of maintenance or none at all. They will be discarded when they no longer function, because it would be as expensive to repair and maintain them as to replace them.

To set the objectives for an effective maintenance programme, it is essential to have the following information about each asset:

- Capital cost
- Estimated life
- Predicted cost of maintenance
- Possible resale value
- Ease and cost of replacement

Factors influencing maintenance programmes

The type and costs of maintenance can be influenced during the planning stages of a new building or the purchasing of new equipment, furnishings or fittings by considering the following points.

Design This includes the ease with which cleaning and maintenance can be carried out.

Construction and materials The method of construction and materials used determines the physical and chemical properties of the fabric of a building, furnishings and equipment. The properties of any item, e.g. durability, selected for a particular purpose must be related to the amount and type of wear and tear it will experience.

Supervision Equipment requiring a minimum of supervision during use and furnishings and fittings requiring a minimum of supervision during maintenance will be preferable.

Planned maintenance programmes

When planning the maintenance programme for any asset, having set the objectives, e.g. planned/controlled deterioration, the aims of the programme should be to:

- Spread the cost of maintenance over the life-cycle of each item.
- Carry out maintenance in the least obtrusive manner possible. For example, in a seasonal hotel bedrooms should be redecorated 'out-of-season'.
- Fulfil any legal requirements and organizational policy about frequency and quality of maintenance.
- Inspect each item regularly and then decide upon any follow-up action which may be necessary.
- Determine the desired frequency of maintenance, based on information from manufacturers, historical records, past experience and own 'informed' estimate.

- Effect the necessary maintenance programme with the minimum expenditure.

During planning consideration must be given to the desirability, cost and efficiency of using contractors.

Factors affecting work planning

Before undertaking the organization of accommodation, cleaning and maintenance services, it is necessary to consider the factors affecting the planning of such work.

Services provided by the organization

The type of organization will determine the range of services required. In a hospital the domestic services department will largely be concerned with cleaning. In a hotel the housekeeping department will be concerned with cleaning, linen and room services.

The use of the building

In order to provide an unobtrusive and effective service, it is necessary to know:

1 Times during which the building is used and, hence, its availability for cleaning and maintenance.
2 Times when other services are required, e.g. food and beverage service.
3 Activities and dirt-making processes carried out, particularly noting processes which create special problems.
4 Degree of congestion.
5 Amount of traffic within the building.
6 Likely future changes in use which will affect the services required.

The standard of service required

It is vital to consult with the consumer of the services to be provided or for the housekeeping and domestic services departments to liaise with other departments in order to agree the standard of service to be provided.

Job priorities

The consumer or other departments should be consulted to enable job priorities to be determined. This assists in maintaining standards of work. In times of emergency, work can be reallocated such that priority jobs are carried out, thus minimizing the effect on standards.

Availability of labour

It is important to consider the availability of labour when planning times and methods of work. An assessment of existing staff and the local labour market should provide information relating to types and skills of staff available, the time at which they are willing to work and the amount of training required to enable them to achieve the correct standards.

Equipment and materials

An evaluation of existing cleaning and maintenance equipment and materials may assist in work planning.

The availability of storage space may affect the type of equipment and materials selected, since effective control may only be facilitated by secure, adequate storage facilities. The availability of a regular and reliable supply of materials and equipment may influence the choice of procedures.

Communication and consultation

The importance of effective communication and consultation with consumers, existing staff and their trade unions throughout all phases of work planning, organization and control cannot be too highly stressed.

Desirability of contract services

Consideration should be given to the availability, cost and standard of services provided by contractors.

Contract services

There is a wide range of contract services available to housekeeping and accommodation services departments. Many firms of reputable contractors can provide either a total cleaning maintenance and domestic service or just one or two specialist services alongside direct labour who carry out the main part of the services.

Types of contract service

Contract service can include all or any of the following:

- Carpet cleaning
- Equipment servicing and maintenance
- Exterior cleaning
- Floor maintenance
- Floral arrangements
- Ground and garden services
- High-level cleaning
- Interior or exterior decoration
- Laundry
- Linen rental
- Pest control
- Plant maintenance
- Security services
- Soft-furnishing cleaning
- Uniform rental
- Wall washing
- Window cleaning

Many large cleaning contractors provide a complete service for hotels, hospitals, hostels, offices, institutional and industrial organizations or will provide part of a combined service of direct and contract labour. For example, in an hotel, the hotel may employ direct labour as room attendants, whilst a contractor may provide a cleaning service for the public areas.

Advantages and disadvantages of contract services

These are tabulated in Table 9 and should be considered before a decision is made to make use of them. However, once the decision has been made to employ the services of a contractor, the

Table 9   *Advantages and disadvantages of contract services*

Advantages	Disadvantages
• Contractors are specialists who can provide thorough training and use the correct equipment	• As the setting up of a contract cleaning and maintenance firm is not subject to any regulations, some contractors may not be specialists
• Managers are relieved of the problems of the housekeeping/domestic management department	• Some elements of control are removed from management
• Risk and hazard to direct labour is reduced, e.g. exterior window-cleaning	• Contract staff may have divided loyalties — to the contractor and to the client
• Extra work may be undertaken without permanent staff increases	• A contract may limit flexibility and so not cater for frequently changing conditions
• Emergency cleaning services may be provided at short notice	• Minimal effort may be used to achieve the maximum profit
• Reduces the need for capital investment in specialized equipment	• The lowest tendered contract price is often accepted, and this may lead to a deterioration of standards
• The contractor, rather than management, deals with problems and industrial relations matters	• Interdepartmental liaison within the client's organization may be reduced
	• There may be security problems

most reputable firm, which will provide the most efficient service to meet the requirements of the client, must be sought. The client will usually advertise and invite contractors to submit a tender for carrying out the required service. In order to do this, the contractor must be provided with access to survey the area of work, all relevant details of the service required and the constraints. Having received all tenders for the work, the client must assess each one and eventually form the contract with the most suitable firm.

Factors to be considered

When a contract cleaning service is to be used, it is important that the contract is made with the company which will provide the most efficient service to meet the client's needs. Unfortunately, contractors have traditionally often been selected because they have submitted the lowest priced tender and, unless it has been ascertained that the quoted price is for the required services, then this practice may lead to a deterioration of standards. It is important to consider the following factors for each contractor under consideration:

- Availability of reference accounts.
- The contractor's experience in the type of service required.
- Financial references.
- Professional qualifications of the contractors.
- Personnel policies.
- Methods of supervision and quality control.

- Type of contract available and method of payment.

Where difficulties arise in the choice of contractor, a cleaning industry consultant will provide an objective view.

Types of contract

There are many methods of pricing a contract, the following are the most commonly used.

Fixed periodic cost This type of contract is frequently used. It undertakes to provide a specified service for a fixed price. It details the frequency and method of providing the service, but does not stipulate manning levels or types of equipment to be used.

Fixed periodic cost with controlled input Similar to the above contract, but it does specify the minimum number of man-hours to be used to provide the service.

Management fee The client provides and pays the wages of the operatives, whilst paying the contractor a fee for the provision of the organization, supervision and management of the contracted service.

Cost plus percentage profit The client pays the cost of a service – which may be both flexible and varied – and also pays the contractor an agreed percentage of the cost of this service, as profit. If this type of contract is used, it is essential that the client controls it carefully, to ensure that an unscrupulous contractor is not increasing costs purely to achieve a greater profit.

Cost plus fixed fee The contractor receives payment for the cost of the service – which may be flexible – plus a fixed, unchanging fee for the provision of the contract service. This type of contract is often the most satisfactory since the service may be varied to meet the changing needs of the client, but there is no incentive for the contractor to increase costs unnecessarily.

Stages in work planning

This section details the various stages that can be employed in work planning. The actual procedure used will depend on the organization, the service to be provided and the situation. Not all stages or documents described will necessarily be used.

The survey

This is a tool that enables the correct and most effective cleaning, maintenance or other service, to be provided within the unavoidable constraints of any room, building or organization. It provides the basis for a methodical approach to organization, costing and control. The survey will involve a number of distinct steps:

Agree objectives with the consumer, client or other departments This will determine the scope of the work/project to be undertaken.

Consultation The consumer, client or other departments must be consulted to:

- Establish working relationships.
- Discuss standard and type of service required.
- Determine the availability and use of the building.
- Determine any special constraints, e.g. financial.

Existing staff and their trade union must be consulted to:

- Inform staff of the project being undertaken and its implications.
- Foster a cooperative attitude.

Standard of service to be achieved must be established. A general policy statement of the standard of work to be carried out should be prepared, even though a consumer may have a poorly defined idea of his requirements. In the case of cleaning services, a variety of terms are used to define the standard required. The standards required and the terms used by different organizations for the various areas of a building are described in Volume 1.

CMS Ltd

Top sheet

CLEANING SURVEY

Name of firm/client: **XYZ Co.**

Address of firm: **Grand Hotel**

Site: **Newtown**

Survey carried out by: **BMW**

Date: **20·7·81**

Sheet no. **1** of **4**

Room: **Residents' Lounge**

Area: **20 × 15·5 metres = 310 m²**

Floor: **New 80% wool, 20% nylon carpet**

Congestion: **Medium**

Floor condition and treatment: **Good condition. No previous treatment.**

Item	No. of units	Frequency	Basic time (min)	Allowances (%)	Standard time (min)	Allowed time (min)
Vacuum carpet	31	7/7	792.05	14	902.94	1200.91
Vacuum carpet edges	7	1/7	25.55	14	29.13	38.74
High dust	31	1/7	196.54	14	224.06	298.00
Damp dust furniture	20	7/7	79.80	14	90.98	121.00

Cleaning survey: **XYZ Co. Grand Hotel, Newtown**

Continuation sheet: No. **2**

Item	No. of units	Frequency	Basic time (min)	Allowances (%)	Standard time (min)	Allowed time (min)
Damp dust chair	4	7/7	14.56	14	16.60	22.08
Damp dust table	7	7/7	34.79	14	39.66	52.74
Damp dust radiator	6	1/7	5.04	14	5.75	7.65

Figure 29 *Example of a cleaning survey*

CMS Ltd

Cleaning Survey

Customer: XYZ Co.
    Grand Hotel,
    Newtown

Telephone: Newtown 5848

Contact: Head Housekeeper

Sheet: **1**   of **4**

Date: 20.7.81

Location: Newtown

Survey sheet: **1**

Client requirements: Daily cleaning

Standard of service: Public and guest areas - Prestige
    Other areas   - General

Time: 6.00 am - 9.00 am

Room or area	Item Type	Item Area or units	Dens	Method and frequency of cleaning		Notes	Allowed time (min)
Residents Lounge	A1	310 m²	M	Suction clean	7/7		1200.91
				Suction clean edges	1/7		38.74
	B1	20		Damp dust	7/7		121.00
	B2	4		Damp dust	7/7		22.09
	B3	20		Suction clean	1/7		106.13
	B4	7		Damp dust	7/7		52.75
	B5	6		Damp dust	1/7		7.64

Sheet: **4**   of **4**

Room or area	Item Type	Item Area or units	Dens	Method and frequency of cleaning		Notes	Allowed time (min)
Lounge Bar	A2	170 m²	H	Suction clean	7/7		615.12
				Suction clean edges	1/7		19.88
	B1	10		Damp wipe	7/7		60.50
	B2	20		Damp wipe	7/7		124.50
	B3	6		Damp wipe	7/7		53.57

Total floor area (m²)	1910	Total time floor and furniture (hr)	55.71
		Daily hours	7.96
		Work performance (m²/hr)	240

Figure 30   *Example of a cleaning survey using codes*

Carry out the survey When undertaking cleaning services, this can be done using standard, preprinted forms such as those given in Figures 29 and 30.

Commence the survey at the main entrance and work round the building in a clockwise direction, surveying each area in turn. Plans must not be relied on because they may be out of date and do not identify surfaces or the degree of congestion. In each room or area the following tasks should be carried out:

1 Measure the floor area using a tape or pedometer. It can be useful to prepare a rough sketch.
2 Identify floor coverings and treatments, noting condition and existing method of maintenance.
3 Estimate wall, ceiling and window areas and identify the type of finish where relevant.
4 Note the degree of congestion. This will affect the ease with which the service can be carried out.
5 Note the availability of power points and water supply. This can affect the type of equipment used and methods employed.
6 Itemize the contents of the room, working from the door in a clockwise direction to avoid oversight or repetition. The types of furniture and fittings and the numbers of each should be

Table 10 *Surveying codes*

Code	Item
A1	1-5 year old Axminster carpet
A2	6-10 year old Axminster carpet
A3	11-20 year old Axminster carpet
A4	Over 20-year-old Axminster carpet
A5	Carpet in need of repair
B1	Cupboards
B2	Chairs
B3	Upholstered chairs
B4	Tables
B5	PVC-upholstered chairs
Sp	Added after normal code to indicate special cleaning

listed. Many organizations have devised their own set of codes to simplify the recording process. Table 10 shows part of a typical method of recording and Figure 30 shows the use of such codes.

For the building as a whole:

a List existing cleaning equipment and materials.
b Determine cleaning storage facilities and services.
c Determine all security requirements.
d Note the environment in which domestic staff will be required to work.
e Identify any special precautions to be observed or any particular hazards.

Consult client or other departments again to discuss and agree type and standard of service, frequencies, special requirements and ad hoc duties.

The specification

Once the survey has been completed it is necessary to prepare a specification. This is a detailed plan showing each area of work, each task within that area and the frequency with which each task is carried out. When preparing a specification for cleaning and maintenance services, the methods employed and the frequency of carrying out each task will be governed by factors described in Volume 1. Routine tasks are usually expressed on a weekly basis and periodic tasks on a monthly, three-monthly, six-monthly or yearly basis. Typical methods of writing down frequencies are:

1/7 once per week	1/52 or 1/2 once per year
3/7 three times per week	2/52 or 2/12 once every 6 months
7/7 daily	4/52 or 4/12 once every 3 months
	6/52 or 6/12 once every 2 months

An example of a specification is shown in Figure 31.

The specification, when agreed by the consumer or other departments, is the basis on which a service is provided and defines the standard of that service. It can subsequently be used to prepare estimates, work schedules and master schedules.

CMS Ltd

Customer: XYZ Co.
                Grand Hotel
                Newtown

Date: 27.7.81

Location: Newtown

Specification No: 1876

Specification: Daily cleaning service of all public areas of hotel

Special requirements:

1   Standard: Guest areas — Prestige
                         Other areas — General

2   Work to be carried out with minimum of disturbance to guests, preferably 6.00 am to 9.00 am.

3   Hotel staff to spot check and clean regularly throughout service in restaurant and bar.

4   Function rooms to be cleaned on day of use; before and after use.

5   Hotel porters to remove waste routinely.

Area	Job	Frequency Routine	Periodic	Need
Residents Lounge	Vacuum carpet	7/7		
Cocktail Bar	Vacuum carpet edges	1/7		
Public Bar	High dust	1/7		
	Damp wipe furniture and fittings	7/7		
	Vacuum upholstery	1/7		
Restaurant	Vacuum carpet	7/7		
Reception	Vacuum carpet edges	1/7		
	High dust	1/7		
	Damp wipe furniture and fittings	7/7		
	Vacuum upholstery	7/7		
Function Rooms	Vacuum carpet			
	Vacuum carpet edges			On day
	High dust			of use
	Damp wipe furniture and fittings			only
	Vacuum upholstery			
Corridors	Vacuum carpets	5/7		
	Vacuum carpet edges		1/12	
	High dust		1/12	
	Damp wipe furniture and fittings	5/7		

Figure 31 *Example of a cleaning specification*

Table 11 *Examples of synthetic data*

Element/task	Unit	Basic time, min	Allowed time, min
Wet mop floor	10 m^2	3.17	4.82
Impregnate mop floor	10 m^2	1.75	2.66
Buff floor	10 m^2	3.17	4.82
Scrub floor	10 m^2	6.89	10.47
High dust	per 10 m^2 floor area	6.34	9.64
Vacuum floor	10 m^2	3.65	5.55
Damp dust furniture	per item	0.57	0.87
Damp dust chair	per item	0.52	0.79
Damp dust desk/table	per item	0.71	1.08
Damp dust equipment	per item	0.41	0.62
Damp dust ledge	per item (0.25 m x 3 m approx.)	0.48	0.73
Damp dust rails	per item (2 cm x 3 m approx.)	0.08	0.12
Damp dust radiator	per item	0.84	1.28
Damp dust door/frame	per item	2.22	3.37
Damp dust miscellaneous items	per item	0.57	0.87
Damp dust bed frame	per item	0.89	1.35
Defrost and clean 'fridge'	per item	16.47	25.03
Clean sink	per item	3.17	4.82
Clean sink unit	per item	5.14	7.81
Clean lavatory basin	per item	1.59	2.42
Clean WC	per item	1.90	2.89
Clean urinal	per item	4.07	6.19
Clean bath	per item	4.25	6.46
Clean mirror	per item (0.5 m x 1 m approx.)	0.71	1.08
Clean venetian blinds	per item (1 m x 2 m approx.)	4.28	6.51
Clean kitchen cupboard	per item	17.48	26.57
Empty waste-paper basket	per item	0.79	1.20
Wash waste-paper basket	per item	2.06	3.13
Clean stairs	per item	0.55	0.84
Wash wall tiles	per 10 m^2 floor area	3.81	5.79
Vacuum rug	per item (1.5 m x 0.75 m)	3.97	6.03
Vacuum mat/well	per item	3.97	6.03
Clean cooker	per item	9.08	13.80

Allowed time and labour requirements

Having completed the survey and specification it is possible to calculate the allowed time and labour required to provide the service. When a service is to be provided for a limited period of time, e.g. the deep cleaning of all carpets in a hotel may only take two days, the total allowed time and time to carry out that service is determined. When a service is provided over a period of time the allowed time is usually calculated on a weekly basis. To determine the allowed time synthetic data is used.

Synthetic data Synthesis is the 'work measurement technique for building up the time for a job or parts of a job at a defined level of performance by totalling element times obtained previously from time studies on other jobs or from synthetic data'. Synthetic data are the times required to carry out various jobs or tasks under specific conditions and to achieve a specified standard of service (see Table 11). They should be basic times, i.e. the time required to carry out a task at the standard level of performance.

To determine the allowed time for a job, allowances will be added to the basic time to give the standard time and a factor applied to the standard time to give the allowed time at the required level of performance. For convenience and where allowances and performances are fixed, data based on allowed times will be used.

Many organizations have their own sets of synthetic data. It is important that data is not transferred from one organization to another if inaccuracies are to be avoided. Inaccuracies can arise because an organization will have derived its datum for carrying out a particular task using particular pieces of equipment and procedures. In another organization the equipment and procedures used for carrying out that task may be different.

Allowances (see Table 12) which may be added to the basic time are as follows.

Relaxation allowances are intended to provide the worker with the opportunity to recover from the physiological and psychological effects of carrying out that job under specified conditions and to allow attention to personal needs. The percentage amount of the allowance will depend on the nature of the work and on local negotiation, although there are tables of percentage allowances available recommended by various management consultants. The allowances for most domestic cleaning work is generally 13 to 16%, and this, and all other allowances, will usually be the subject of local negotiation.

Contingency allowances are included in the time allowed for a job to meet legitimate and expected items of work or delays which cannot be accurately measured because of their irregular occurrence.

Special allowances may be given for any activities not normally part of the operation of the job but which are necessary to carry out the job satisfactorily.

Table 12 *Calculation of relaxation allowances, given as percentages of basic times*

	Men	*Women*
Constant allowances:		
Personal needs	5	7
Basic fatigue	4	4
	9	11
Variable additions to constant allowances:		
Standing allowance	2	2
Abnormal position	0-7	1-7
Light conditions	2-5	2-5
Air conditions	5-15	5-15
Visual strain	2-5	2-5
Aural strain	2-5	2-5
Mental strain	1-8	1-8
Monotony, mental	1-4	1-4
Monotony, physical	2-5	1-2
Use of force	Varies in proportion to amount of force exerted	

Learning allowances may be given to trainees until they develop the necessary skills and speeds.

Training allowances may be given to a qualified worker who has to instruct trainees.

Work performance This is an observer's assessment of the pace at which a 'qualified' worker carries out a job, compared with the observer's idea of a standard pace acceptable for that same job. Acceptable performance levels for jobs are usually negotiated locally.

Work performance is important as it provides a measure of the utilization of staff. It may be measured in terms of a scale or in the amount of work done in unit time. For example:

1 On the BS 0–100 scale, where 100 is the standard performance level for a job, a 75 performance is a well motivated, non-bonus level pace. If staff achieve a higher rating on this scale, they may be eligible, depending on local agreement, for a bonus payment. If staff achieve a lower rating on this scale, they will not be achieving the required time or quality standard for the work and so corrective action, e.g. further training, must be taken to enable the established standard to be achieved in the correct time. The assessment of performance will be based upon the time taken to achieve the correct standard of work.

2 Maintenance of 250 m² of floor space per hour may be set as the non-bonus level of performance. If less work is done, corrective action will be necessary. If more work is done, workers may qualify for a bonus payment.

When calculating the allowed time for a job, the allowed time must be reduced proportionately if a higher performance is required and increased if a lower performance is required.

The concept of work performance is based on the 'qualified worker', someone who has the necessary physical attributes, who possesses the required intelligence and education and has the necessary skill and knowledge to carry out the work in hand to satisfactory standards of safety, quantity and quality. The following attributes help to identify the experienced, qualified worker:

- Smooth, consistent movements.
- Rhythm.
- Rapid response to signals.
- Anticipation of difficulties and more ready to overcome them.
- Relaxed, with little appearance of conscious attention.

It is important to base performance levels on the 'qualified' worker, and ideally on the 'average qualified worker', otherwise too much time may be allocated to a task.

There are a number of factors affecting the pace of work. Those outside the worker's control include:

1 Variations in the quality of materials used.
2 Changes in the operating efficiency of tools and equipment within their useful life.
3 Minor or unavoidable changes in methods or conditions of work.
4 Changes in environmental conditions, e.g. lighting or temperature.
5 Variations in mental attention.

Factors within the worker's control include:

1 Variations due to ability.
2 Variations due to attitude of mind, particularly attitude to the organization for which he works.
3 Acceptable variations in the quality of the product.

The optimum pace at which a worker will perform depends on:

1 The physical effort demanded by the job.
2 The care required on the part of the worker.
3 His training and experience.

Stages in the calculation of allowed time to provide a service A practical example of the various stages is shown in Figure 29. The data in Table 11 are used.

1 *Calculation of basic time for each type of task* The basic time is determined from the following formula:

Basic time =   Number of items ×
                Synthetic time/unit × frequency

or

Basic time =   Area of item ×
                Synthetic time/unit × frequency

Synthetic time will be obtained from tables. The frequency of a task provided in a once-only service will be the number of times that task is performed in providing the service. In the case of a service provided over a period of time the frequency with which the task is performed per week is normally used. If the frequency is less than weekly it will still be expressed per week, e.g. the frequency of a task performed four times per year will be four divided by 52 (weeks).

2   *Calculation of standard time for each type of task*   The standard time is determined from the following formula:

Standard time = Basic time + Allowances
                        (% of basic time)

Allowances should be added to the basic time for each task in a series of tasks and not added to the total basic time for all the tasks.

3   *Calculation of allowed time for each type of task*
The allowed time is determined from the formula:

Allowed time =   Standard time × R

Where R is equal to

$$\frac{\text{Rating for a standard performance}}{\text{Rating for the required performance}}$$

For example, the allowed time at a 75 performance, for a standard time of 100 min will be

$$100 \times (100/75) = 133 \text{ min}$$

When 'synthetic data' for allowed times can be used, the calculation of the allowed times for each type of task is simplified, the calculations of standard and allowed times having already been carried out. For each task the 'synthetic' allowed time is multiplied by the number of units and the frequency with which each task is carried out.

4   *Calculation of total allowed time*   The total allowed time for the provision of a service is determined by adding together the allowed times for each task in the service.

Calculation of labour requirements   The number of operative staff required to provide a service can sometimes be simply determined from the relationship given below (although it may be necessary to make an allowance for work carried out by a supervisor):

Number of operatives = A/N

Where A is the allowed time and N the number of hours work by each operative. More frequently, however, particularly where service is provided over a period of time and involves a wide range of different tasks, it is preferable to determine the number of staff and the number of hours each will work when preparing work and master schedules. In such situations the number of operatives and other staff will be governed by availability of rooms for servicing, differences in the frequency with which different tasks are performed, the time allowed to perform different tasks and the number of operatives required to carry them out. Allowances for holidays and travelling times will also affect the number of operatives required.

As a simplified example, the total weekly time for routine work might be 600 hr, including time for preparation, cleaning and maintenance of equipment. Initially it could appear that this work can be undertaken by 15 full-time staff working 40 hr per week. However, after work scheduling, it may become apparent that the work could most efficiently be carried out by 5 full-time staff working normal shifts, 5 full-time staff working split shifts and 10 part-time staff working 20 hr each per week. To this must be added an allowance for holidays, say 10%, bringing the total number of staff required to carry out routine daily work to 11 full-time and 11 part-time staff.

The method of determining the number of staff to undertake periodic work will depend on the amount of such work, its type and frequency. For example, where there is little such work it may simply be added as overtime to the work of staff involved in daily routine work. Where the amount of periodic work warrants it, and it can be scheduled to provide regular balanced work loads, additional full- or part-time staff should be employed.

Estimates of total work performance

The allowed time for a service can be used to calculate the overall work performance which will be achieved. When providing a cleaning service it is expressed in square metres per hour and is a measure of the area of floor and associated furniture and fittings cleaned or serviced per hour. It can be used for walls or windows. It is calculated from the formula:

Work performance = A/T

Where A is the total area to be cleaned or serviced and T is the daily hours or total allowed time. For a once-only service, total allowed time will be used in the calculation. Daily hours are used where the service is provided on a continuing basis and is the total allowed time per week divided by the number of days per week when the service is provided (see Figure 30).

It should be appreciated that a high work performance figure can be indicative of one of two things:

1 A lower standard of service which requires less time.
2 A high standard of service carried out more efficiently.

The actual work performance which should be achieved in particular areas of hospitals, hotels and residential establishments depends on the areas concerned and the standard required. However it will broadly range from about 50 to 300 m²/hr, the higher the required standard the lower the work performance figure. Nevertheless, the objective is always to achieve the highest possible figure within the unavoidable constraints of the situation.

Equipment and materials requirements

If a survey and specification are to be used for estimating purposes, then it will be necessary at this stage to determine equipment and materials required to perform a service. If not, they can be determined when preparing the work schedule. The type of equipment and materials required will depend on the service to be provided. The selection of those for cleaning is described in Volume 1.

The work schedule

Once the time allowed to provide the required type and standard of service has been calculated, work schedules can be prepared. It may also be known as the job schedule, cleaning schedule or maintenance schedule. It is an important stage in the planning process. Its main advantages are that it can be used to:

1 Assist in the establishment and maintenance of the standard of service required.
2 Assist in the organization and allocation of work.
3 Determine equipment and materials requirements.
4 Determine labour requirements.
5 Provide a basis for controlling the cost and quality of the work.
6 Aid communication by making information available to all staff.
7 Assist in the training of staff.
8 Assist in the implementation of incentive bonus schemes.

The actual detail in the schedule is frequently tailored to suit particular situations (see Figures 32 and 33 for examples).

In the case of cleaning services, at its most detailed, it can include:

- Areas or work locations.
- Tasks to be carried out.
- Frequency of tasks.
- Time allowed.
- When each task will be carried out.
- Cleaning agents.
- Cleaning equipment.

Room	Clinic 1	Clinic 2	Clinic 3
Pram park		Dust control mop ODU Wet mop ODU Scrub 1/4 weeks	Dust control mop 2/7 Wet mop 1/7 Scrub 1/8 weeks
Foyer	Dust control mop 3/7 Wet mop 2/7 Buff 1/7 Scrub 1/8 weeks	Dust control mop ODU Wet mop ODU Scrub 1/4 weeks	
Play room			Dust control mop ODU Wet mop ODU Buff 3/7 Scrub 1/4 weeks
Waiting room	Dust control mop 3/7 Wet mop 2/7 Buff 1/7	Dust control mop ODU Wet mop ODU Buff 3/7	Dust control mop ODU Wet mop ODU Buff 1/7
Corridor		Dust control mop ODU Wet mop ODU Buff 3/7 Scrub 1/4 weeks	Dust control mop ODU Wet mop ODU Buff 3/7
Reception			Dust control mop ODU Wet mop ODU Buff 2/7 Scrub 1/4 weeks
Treatment room	Dust control mop 3/7 Wet mop 2/7 Buff 1/7 Scrub 1/8 weeks	Dust control mop ODU Wet mop ODU Buff 3/7 Scrub 1/4 weeks	Dust control mop ODU Wet mop ODU Scrub 1/4 weeks
Consulting room	Dust control mop 3/7 Wet mop 2/7 Buff 1/7 Scrub 1/8 weeks	Dust control mop ODU Wet mop ODU Buff 3/7 Scrub 1/4 weeks	Vacuum ODU

Key

ODU — on day of use
1/7 — once per week
3/7 — three times per week
1/4 weeks — once per four weeks
1/8 weeks — once per eight weeks

Figure 32 *Work schedule for clinic floors*

Report presentation

Following the preparation of a specification, calculation of allowed times and determination of the equipment and materials required it will be possible to prepare a report detailing the service to be provided and the cost. Costing is discussed on pages 86–9. The report will be submitted to the client, other departments, existing staff, etc., as appropriate. Each organization will have its own standard format for such a report.

Work allocation

Once the work scheduling has been completed, work allocation can begin. There are three main methods of allocation. Arrangements will also have to be made to deal with emergencies and overtime.

Traditional method (also known as the unit method)   Each area of the building is allocated a member/members of staff, who always work on that area and carry out all the work on that area. For example, in a residential establishment a cleaner may be allocated 15 rooms to service within a particular area of the establishment. The staff are therefore multi-skilled. This method makes staff more flexible, provides them with a strong sense of 'identity' and 'belonging' and enables them to take a pride in caring for their

Area	Floor/ Furniture	Jobs	Units	Frequency	Time (min/wk)	Days(s)	Time (min/day)	Materials	Equipment
Residents Lounge	A1 (310 m²)	Suction clean		7/7	1200.94	Daily	171.56	–	Vacuum cleaner
		Suction clean edges		1/7	38.74	Monday	38.74	–	Vacuum cleaner and carpet edge tool
	B1	Damp wipe	20	7/7	121.00	Daily	17.29	Neutral synthetic detergent	Bucket, bucket cloth swabs
	B2	Damp wipe	4	7/7	22.09	Daily	3.16		
	B4	Damp wipe	7	7/7	52.75	Daily	7.54		
	B5	Damp wipe	6	1/7	7.64	Monday	7.64		
	B3	Suction clean	20	1/7	106.13	Tuesday	106.13	–	Vacuum cleaner and upholstery and crevice tool
	C7	High dust	31	1/7	340.57	Wed/Thur/Fri	113.52	–	Wall mop, step ladders, dusters
	D5	Damp wipe and buff	4	1/7	14.27	Monday	14.27	Neutral synthetic detergent	Swabs, dry duster
					1904.13 min				

Total hours per week	31.75
Number of operatives	2

Figure 33 *Part of a work schedule*

own areas of work. Within a large workforce there will usually be a 'relief' team, usually composed of new and trainee staff, who fill in and cover the work of the staff who are absent (holidays, sickness, etc.).

Occasionally this method of organizing staff is used to provide extra motivation or discipline, e.g. the promise of 'promotion' from the relief team to a permanent job or threat of 'demotion' from a permanent job back to the relief team when work is unsatisfactory.

Team method (also known as the functional method). The workforce is divided into a number of teams, each team specializing in one type of cleaning work, e.g. floor maintenance, bathroom cleaning and general cleaning. Each team progresses through the building, performing only its own limited range of jobs. The work has to be carefully planned to ensure coordination of the work of each team. It may be helpful to stagger the starting times of each team to eliminate delays.

Within this method, staff are specialists in a limited range of skills, which may reduce their versatility and flexibility. Boredom may result unless the work of the teams is rotated, but good team spirit may be promoted. Many establishments employ a modified form of the traditional and team approaches, e.g. one regular member of staff carrying out general cleaning in each area plus a floor-maintenance team, which carries out floor-maintenance throughout the building.

Block or column cleaning   In this method of work allocation the workforce is directed to concentrate all its resources and efforts into cleaning one block area or floor of a building at a time. The first block is completely serviced before the second block is commenced.

With this method, staff may be multi-skilled or may each have a specialist skill. Control can be easier in many ways, in that the supervisor should always know where to find all staff at any given time. It should also promote 'team spirit' and good communications within the domestic department or cleaning team. The method is probably most satisfactory where the cleaning service is provided whilst consumers are absent, or where there is no necessity for a member of domestic staff to be on duty in an area throughout the working day. It can also result in significant fuel savings particularly when cleaning multistorey buildings.

Emergencies   When these occur, e.g. large-scale absenteeism or extra, unavoidable work as a result of flood damage, there may be insufficient staff to cover all available work. Supervisors must deal with this problem immediately and usually adopt a variety of methods to cope with the situation:

1   Allocate available staff to priority jobs.
2   Cover available work themselves and neglect supervision.
3   Allocate double/triple work loads to staff.
4   Allow staff to carry out normal duties only, neglecting many areas of work.

The first method is the most satisfactory way of coping with emergencies.

Priority jobs should have been identified, defined and agreed with both staff and consumer so that if an emergency arises, supervisors can easily re-allocate work with a minimum of effect on the standard of service.

Overtime should only be used for special tasks which cannot be carried out within the normal work programme, e.g. commissioning a new building or as a temporary measure for covering staff shortages.

Where work schedules and specifications have been effectively drawn up, it is relatively easy to check that no one employee claims overtime to complete their allotted work. Constant covering or overtime often means that the work has not been correctly planned and must therefore be corrected.

The master schedule

The master schedule is a document showing the work allocated to each operative or group of operatives in a building or group of buildings. Figures 34 and 35 show two different formats of a master schedule for routine work. Figure 36 shows the stages in the planning of a master schedule for periodic wall washing and part of the schedule.

Depending on the organization and situation, periodic tasks may be scheduled in several ways:

1   Allocated to form part of the schedule for routine work.
2   Carried out as overtime.
3   Scheduled separately from routine work and carried out either by contractors or staff not normally involved in routine work.

Routine and periodic work should be scheduled to provide a balanced work load for staff, spreading work throughout the week or year as appropriate.

A copy of an individual operative's work may be given to him or her as an *aide-mémoire* and should be posted in their cupboard or work area. Full implementation of required standards can only be achieved if the operative has this knowledge, understands his job and has been trained to carry out the work correctly within the allowed time. Documents which will assist operatives to complete their work to the required standard include order-of-work cards and job routines.

Order-of-work cards   These are pocket-sized cards which detail the necessary cleaning equipment, cleaning agent and method of work

Operative	Location	Job	Frequency	
			Day	Time
B + C	1a	Scrub floor	Monday	2.00→4.00
	1b	Spray clean		4.00−4.30
	1c	Spray clean		4.30−4.50
	HMC	Clean and store equipment		4.50−5.00
	Off-duty			5.00
	2	Light scrub and buff floor	Tuesday	2.00−4.50
	HMC	Clean and store equipment		4.50−5.00
	Off-duty			5.00
	3a	Spray clean floors	Wednesday	2.00−2.20
	3b			2.25−2.45
	3c			2.50−3.10
	3d			3.15−3.45
	3e			3.50−4.10
	3f			4.15−4.45
	HMC	Clean and store equipment		4.50−5.00
	Off-duty			5.00
	4	Light scrub and buff floor	Thursday	2.00−4.50
	HMC	Clean and store equipment		4.50−5.00
	Off-duty			5.00
	5a	Scrub floor	Friday	2.00−2.45
	5b	Light scrub and buff floor		2.45−3.30
	5c	Spray clean floor		3.35−4.30
	5d	Spray clean floor		4.35−4.50
	HMC	Clean and store equipment		4.50−5.00
	Off-duty			5.00

Figure 34 *Example of a master schedule for routine work (1)*

for either a specific item, e.g. daily cleaning of a telephone or a bath, or for cleaning a whole room, e.g. daily cleaning of a bedroom or spring cleaning of a lounge. Because of their convenient size staff can carry these in their overall pockets for easy reference. An example is shown in Figure 37.

Job routines These are large printed sheets which are posted inside the attendant or cleaner's cupboard door for ease of reference. They contain similar information to order-of-work cards. An example is shown in Figure 38.

Duty rotas

Rotas or rosters will often be used to show hours of duty, area of work and days off. They are frequently used where staff work shifts. An example is shown in Figure 39.

Control of standards

The work specification, work schedule and master schedules provide detailed information of the member of staff. Training, order-of-work cards and job routines will ensure each operative or attendant knows what has to be done, when, how to carry out each task and the time allowed. Routine and periodic inspection of work carried

Operative	Work location	Jobs	Time	Frequency				
				M	T	W	T	F
A	1	Remove waste	7.00 a.m.	1	1	1	1	1
		Damp dust	7.15 a.m.	1	1	1	1	1
		Dust control mop floor	7.45 a.m.	1	1	1	1	1
		Wet mop floor	8.00 a.m.	1	1	1	1	1
		Set out chairs	8.30 a.m.	1	1	1	1	1
	2	Remove waste	8.50 a.m.	1		1		1
		Damp dust	9.00 a.m.	1		1		1
		Dust control mop floor	9.10 a.m.	1		1		1
		Wet mop floor	9.15 a.m.	1		1		1
	3	Remove waste	8.50 a.m.		1		1	
		Damp dust	9.00 a.m.		1		1	
		Polish furniture	9.10 a.m.		1		1	
		Vacuum carpet	9.20 a.m.		1		1	
	4	Strip beds	9.40 a.m.	1	1	1	1	1
		Remove waste	9.50 a.m.	1	1	1	1	1
		Make beds	10.00 a.m.	1	1	1	1	1
		Damp dust	10.12 a.m.	1	1	1	1	1
		Vacuum carpet	10.20 a.m.	1	1	1	1	1
	Break		10.30 a.m.					
	5	Strip beds	10.50 a.m.	1	1	1	1	1
		Remove waste	11.00 a.m.	1	1	1	1	1
		Make beds	11.10 a.m.	1	1	1	1	1
		Damp dust	11.22 a.m.	1	1	1	1	1
		Vacuum carpet	11.30 a.m.	1	1	1	1	1
	6	Remove waste	11.40 a.m.	1	1	1	1	1
		Damp dust	12.00 noon	1	1	1	1	1
		Vacuum carpet	12.10 p.m.	1	1	1	1	1
	HMC	Return equipment to store, clean and dry	12.20 p.m.	1	1	1	1	1
	Off-duty		12.30 p.m.					

Figure 35 *Example of a master schedule for routine work (2)*

Wall Washing in School XYZ

Area	*Treatment*
Offices, corridors, storerooms	Wash once annually
Classrooms 1—10	Wash twice annually
Gymnasium, hall, dining room	Wash three times annually
Classrooms 11—15	Wash four times annually
Toilet areas, kitchens	Wash twelve times annually

Plan

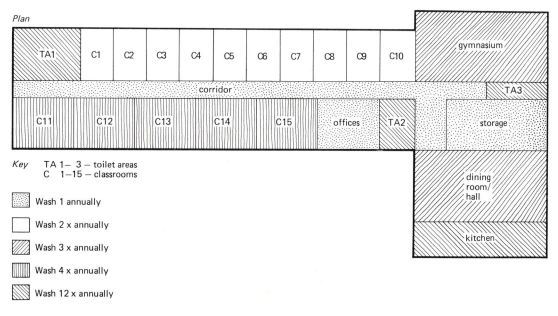

Key TA 1— 3 — toilet areas
     C 1—15 — classrooms

- Wash 1 annually
- Wash 2 x annually
- Wash 3 x annually
- Wash 4 x annually
- Wash 12 x annually

Once these plans have been drawn up, the actual date that each area of work commences and its duration can be timetabled.

Wall Washing Schedule School XYZ:

Date work commences	Date work to be completed	Area	Special notes
1. 8.81	1. 8.81	TA1	Remove graffiti
2. 8.81	2. 8.81	C1, C2	
3. 8.81	3. 8.81	C3, C4	
4. 8.81	4. 8.81	C5, C6	
5. 8.81		C7, C8	

Figure 36 *Example of a maintenance schedule*

```
┌─────────────────────────────────────────────────────────┐
│                                                         │
│        ORDER OF WORK FOR THE SPECIAL CLEAN OF A TELEPHONE │
│                                                         │
│     1  Collect equipment and materials; dry duster, swabs, neutral │
│        synthetic detergents, disinfectants, buckets.    │
│                                                         │
│     2  Wring swab out in detergent solution until barely damp. │
│                                                         │
│     3  Wipe all surfaces of telephone, paying particular attention │
│        to dial, ear and mouth-piece.                    │
│                                                         │
│     4  Wipe flex.                                       │
│                                                         │
│     5  Dry all surfaces with dry duster.                │
│                                                         │
│     6  Wipe ear and mouth-piece with disinfectant solution. │
│                                                         │
│     7  Replace handset on cradle.                       │
│                                                         │
│     8  Check work.                                      │
│                                                         │
└─────────────────────────────────────────────────────────┘
```

Figure 37 *Example of an order-of-work card*

Area: Ward 1   Staff: Domestic assistant A
                                                               Domestic assistant B

                                                       Time: 7.00 a.m. – 1.30 p.m.

Time	Domestic assistant A	Domestic assistant B
7.00 a.m.	Wash dishes, tidy kitchen	Prepare breakfast trays
7.15 a.m.	Make breakfast beverages, prepare serving trolley	
7.30 a.m.	Assist with breakfast service	Assist with breakfast service
7.45 a.m.	Put away milk and kitchen stores	Prepare cleaning equipment
8.00 a.m.	Collect breakfast trays	Collect breakfast trays
8.10 a.m.	Wash breakfast dishes, clean and tidy kitchen	Wash breakfast dishes, clean and tidy kitchen
8.30 a.m.	Remove litter and tidy ward	Remove litter and tidy ancillary rooms
9.00 a.m.	Damp dust ward furniture and fittings	Damp dust ancillary room furniture and fittings
9.30 a.m.	Dust control mop ward floor	Dust control mop ancillary area floors
9.45 a.m.	Damp mop ward floor	Damp mop ancillary area floors
10.15 a.m.	Break	Prepare mid-morning drink
10.30 a.m.	Serve mid-morning drink	Break
10.45 a.m.	Collect used crockery	Collect used crockery
10.50 a.m.	Wash and put away crockery	Wash and put away crockery
11.00 a.m.	Clean bathroom and sluice areas 1–4	Clean bathroom and sluice areas 5–8
11.30 a.m.	Spot check/clean ward areas	Spot check/clean ancillary areas
11.45 a.m.	Clean and store cleaning equipment	Clean and store cleaning equipment
12.00 noon	Prepare trolley and utensils for luncheon service	Prepare trays for luncheon service
12.15 p.m.	Prepare accompaniments to luncheon	Prepare beverages to accompany luncheon
12.30 p.m.	Assist in the service of luncheon	Assist in the service of luncheon
12.45 p.m.	Collect and wash crockery and cutlery	Collect and wash crockery and cutlery
1.00 p.m.	Clean trolley, return containers to kitchen	Clean and tidy kitchen
1.15 p.m.	Spot check/clean ward area	Spot check/clean bathroom areas
1.30 p.m.	Off duty	Off duty

Figure 38 *Example of a job routine*

Work commencing: 4.5.81   7.00 a.m. — 4.00 p.m.

Area	Monday	Tuesday	Wednesday	Thursday	Friday	Saturday	Sunday
1	Joan	Joan	Joan	Joan	Joan	Susan (R)	Susan (R)
2	Thelma (R)	Mary	Mary	Mary	Mary	Mary	Thelma (R)
3	Jean	Karen (R)	Karen (R)	Jean	Jean	Jean	Jean
4	Pat	Pat	Susan (R)	Susan (R)	Pat	Pat	Pat
5	Alice	Alice	Alice	Karen (R)	Karen (R)	Alice	Alice
6	Carol	Carol	Carol	Carol	Thelma (R)	Thelma (R)	Carol
7	Pauline	Pauline	Pauline	Pauline	Pauline	Brenda (R)	Brenda (R)
8	Margaret (R)	Julie	Julie	Julie	Julie	Julie	Margaret (R)
9	Brenda (R)	Brenda (R)	Sandra	Sandra	Sandra	Sandra	Sandra
10	Grace	Margaret (R)	Margaret (R)	Grace	Grace	Grace	Grace
11	Hannah	Hannah	Brenda (R)	Margaret (R)	Hannah	Hannah	Hannah
12	Millie	Millie	Millie	Thelma (R)	Susan (R)	Millie	Millie
Relief	Karen	—	—	—	—	—	—

Relief team days off:

Susan — Monday, Tuesday
Thelma — Tuesday, Wednesday
Brenda — Thursday, Friday
Margaret — Friday, Saturday
Karen — Saturday, Sunday

Figure 39 *Example of a duty rota*

out and of the fabric, furniture and fittings of a building will then be required.

Routine inspection of work

Routine inspection will be required to:

- Ensure that the correct procedures and methods are used and to correct any faults.
- Ensure that standards are maintained.
- Allow action to be taken to correct defective work to either maintain standards or health and safety.
- Identify responsibility for defective work.
- Enable complaints to be dealt with effectively.

The supervisor should check each employee's work on each area of work at least twice during a work period. The first check should be at the beginning of the work to ensure that it has been started on time and that it is being carried out satisfactorily. The second check should be made before the work in each area has been completed, to ensure that the work is satisfactory and to instruct the operative to correct any faults if necessary. It is also important to check that the work is being achieved in the allowed time.

Checks should not be carried out at exactly the same time each day. Staff would soon be able to predict the arrival time of the supervisor and react accordingly. Spot checks in the course of the work period are useful.

When an operative is inexperienced or unreliable, more frequent checks will be necessary for further training and instruction.

Time/quality control checklists

When checking domestic work, memory alone should not be relied upon; a checklist provides a more thorough, systematic method of checking. Examples are shown in Figures 40 and 41. By maintaining checklists, noting the time when areas have been checked and the name of the person checking, the departmental manager will have information to:

- Assist in ensuring that the work is being

Room/area: Date:

		Satisfactory	Unacceptable
Floor	dust control mop		
	wet mop		
	buff		
	scrub		
Dusting	high		
	low		
	furniture		
	equipment		
	ledges		
	rails		
	radiators		
	bed frames		
	venetian blinds		
Waste bins	empty		
	wash		
Carpet	vacuum edges		
Curtains	neat, tidy		

Work carried out by: Comments:

Work checked by:

Date: Time:

Figure 40 *Example of a quality control chart*

Room: 105

	Housekeeping		Maintenance		
	Satisfactory	Not Satisfactory	Satisfactory	Fault	Action
Floor					
dust control mop	✓				
wet mop	✓				
buff					
scrub					
Dusting					
high		✓			
furniture	✓		✓		
equipment	✓		✓		
ledges	✓		✓		
rails	✓		✓		
radiators	✓		✓		
beds		✓	✓		
blinds		✓		roller action jammed	maintenance dept. to repair immediately
Waste Bin					
empty	✓				
wash		✓			
Carpet					
vacuum	✓			frayed edges	carpet fitter to bind edges
edges	✓				
Light fittings			✓		
Electrical sockets			✓	doorknob missing	maintenance dept. to replace immediately
Door furniture					

Work carried out by: *M. Jones.*   Date: 12/6/82

Work checked by: *J. Smith*   Time: 11.00

Figure 41 *Example of a quality control and maintenance checklist*

carried out and that nothing is being overlooked.
- Show responsibility for both carrying out the work and its supervision.
- Deal with complaints. It is difficult to deal with the complaints from memory only.

A general maintenance check may be built into this type of checklist.

Periodic quality control

This should be carried out by a higher-level supervisor or manager at least once per month in every area of work. It will:

- Establish that correct quality and time standards are being achieved.
- Ensure that supervisors and managers measure to the same standards.
- Establish operative development, needs and performance.
- Foster awareness of the quality of the work.
- Assist with improving morale and motivation of staff.

It is important that work scheduling be flexible, and should be constantly reviewed to ensure that the correct standards are being achieved and that those standards remain appropriate. Informal review during inspection will highlight areas that require a more formal investigation and review, so that rescheduling may take place if necessary.

General maintenance

Regular inspection of the fabric, furniture and fittings of a building is essential to:

- Prevent deterioration of the fabric, etc.

- Maintain standards of appearance.
- Maintain safety standards.
- Reduce the costs of cleaning and maintenance.

When carrying out regular inspections to determine the state and necessary maintenance of an area of a building or item of equipment, preprinted forms should be used to ensure that nothing is missed, to provide a record of faults and necessary maintenance and to provide a further reference. Figure 42 shows part of a typical maintenance checklist showing locations, items of fabric, etc., status of each item and action to be taken.

Following an inspection, a written request should be sent to the relevant department indicating the work to be carried out. It is essential that the department which will carry out the work indicates when it will be started and completed. This will allow action to be taken if work is not completed by the specified date.

Budgeting and costing

A budget is a statement of the expected expenditure and revenue of an organization or department within an organization for a fixed period of time. It will be required to calculate the

Room	Item	Possible faults	Immediate action	Long-term action
1	**Electrical appliances:**			
	Bedside lamp	—	—	—
	Centre light	frayed flex	replace flex	check and replace all flexes of similar age
	Radio	poor reception	check installation	plan replacement
	TV	—	—	—
	Electric heater	faulty element	take out of use replace element and service	—
	Furniture:			
	Bedside table	door hinge broken	replace hinge	—

Figure 42 *Example of part of a maintenance checklist*

cost of services provided and as a basis for financial control through the comparison of actual and budgeted expenditure.

The methods of costing and budgeting described are largely based on absorption costing techniques but it should be appreciated that methods based on techniques known as marginal costing can have advantages over the former, particularly in commercial situations.

Preparation of a budget

Activity levels In a non-commercial organization the range and standard of services to be provided will ideally be determined before the preparation of a budget commences. In practice, financial constraints can limit the services an organization may wish to provide and the range and standard of service will be determined by the amount of money an organization is able to allocate to each department.

In a commercial organization the activity level, i.e. the number of units of service sold, will be determined by market forces and will be less easy to define. It will therefore be necessary to predict the level of activity during the period for which the budget is to apply. Estimates of revenue and expenditure can be made for the level of activity predicted. However, the budget must be capable of responding to changes in levels of activity and must, therefore, be flexible.

Costs The costs involved in the provision of a service and which must be included in a budget will be either direct or indirect (see Table 13) and may be fixed or variable. Direct costs are those items of expenditure which can be attributed to a particular job or department and will be incurred as a result of that job or the services provided by that department. Indirect costs are those costs also referred to as overheads. They are items of expenditure which cannot be attributed to a particular job or department providing a service and will be incurred as a result of the general activities required to run an organization, e.g. the expenses incurred in running a head office will be indirect costs.

When determining the total cost of a job or of the services provided by a department, a proportion of the indirect costs incurred by the whole organization must be added to the direct costs. The actual proportion will depend on the relative contribution that the job or department is expected to make to the overall level of activity of the organization, e.g. if the services provided by a particular department form 10% of the total direct costs of an organization, 10% of the indirect costs should be charged to that department. However, when fixing the selling price of a service, the proportion of indirect costs applied to the direct costs of that service may be governed by other factors, e.g. a particular service may only form 10% of the services sold by a company but a selling price might be fixed that enables 20% of companies' indirect costs to be recovered. This may allow another service to be priced more competitively.

Fixed costs are those costs incurred irrespective of the activity level. They will include the majority of indirect costs and some direct costs, e.g. salaries of department managers.

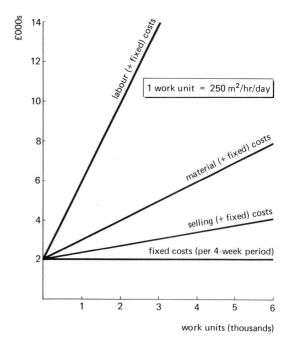

Figure 43 *Example of a variable expenses budget*

Table 13 *Direct and indirect costs*

Type	Expenditure item	Examples
Direct	Labour	Operatives, attendants, supervisors and possibly managers
	Equipment and materials	Linen, food, cleaning equipment and materials, spares, servicing
	Statutory payments	Pensions, NIC
	Miscellaneous	Holidays, transport
	Fuel	Electricity, gas
	Services provided by contractors or other departments	Maintenance, window cleaning, wall washing
Indirect	Labour	Directors, managers, senior supervisors, clerks, typists, sales staff, accounting staff
	Premises and plant	Rent, rates, heat, light, water
	General administration	Stationery, typewriters, data- and word-processing equipment, management services
	Statutory payments	NIC, Pensions
	Selling expenses	Advertising
	Miscellaneous	Holidays, transport, fringe benefits

Variable costs are those costs which vary according to the level of activity. They will include the majority of direct costs and some indirect costs, e.g. selling expenses.

Fixed and flexible budgets A fixed budget is used when the maximum level of expenditure is fixed for the period to which the budget applies. Typically each department will be allocated a specific amount of money which in turn will be allocated to each of the different expenses incurred by the department, e.g. labour, materials.

A flexible budget will be used where expenditure and revenue of a department or organization depends on the level of activity and on changes in that level which might be expected to occur. It will, however, fix the level of expenditure for each item of expense at the various levels of activity. The graph in Figure 43 shows the changes in variable expenses (labour, materials and selling) which might occur in an organization as the activity level increases. Activity is measured in work units, each unit corresponding to the cleaning and maintenance of 250 m² of floor space and associated furniture and fittings per hour per day. At any level of activity expected labour, material and selling costs can be determined from the graph, e.g. if the level of activity is 3,000 units, the respective costs will be £12,000, £3,000 and £1,000.

Budgetary control

Comparison of the actual expenditure and revenue with the budget for a department, job or organization is an important tool in assessing performance. It will highlight any significant differences between actual and budgeted expenditure for any item enabling corrective action to be initiated. Figure 44 shows part of budgetary control report for a department in an organization using a fixed budget and Figure 45 shows an example of similar reports used where flexible budgeting is required and using the data in Figure 43. In this example a simplified technique has been adopted for calculating departures from budget (variances). In practice, more sophisticated techniques can be used.

Budgets will generally be prepared in advance for a 12-month period. However, changes in conditions may make it necessary to alter a budget in order to make it more meaningful in terms of prevailing conditions, e.g. an increase in labour costs. Periodic reviews should therefore be undertaken.

Calculating the cost and selling price of a service

When determining the cost or preparing an estimate for a department or service, the method employed will depend on the degree of accuracy required, the type of service being provided and the prevailing market conditions. Whatever method is used, the cost must reflect all costs involved, both direct and indirect.

Costing a specific service or job   This will involve determining the likely expenditure on each item of direct cost. To the total direct cost will be added a percentage to cover indirect costs and percentages for profit and VAT if applicable. The costs to be included are shown in Table 14. An example will serve to illustrate the main points. Consider the cost of cleaning and maintaining 1,000 m² of carpet per annum:

Dept: Housekeeping				Date: 31 June 1981		
Expense item		*June*			*Year to date*	
	Actual	*Budget*	*Variance*	*Actual*	*Budget*	*Variance*
Labour	1,100	1,000	(100)	3,200	3,500	300
Cleaning materials	100	90	(10)	250	240	(10)
Total	1,600	1,400	(200)	4,500	4,550	(50)

Figure 44   *Budgetary control report (fixed budget)*

Department/job: Office cleaning				Date: 31 June 1981		
Unit: 250 m²/hour/day				Unit sales value: £7		
		Period 3 (June)			*Year to date*	
	Actual	*Budget*	*Variance*	*Actual*	*Budget*	*Variance*
Number of units	*800*	*1,000*	*(200)*	*2,400*	*3,000*	*(600)*
Value	5,600	7,000	(1400)	16,800	21,000	(4,200)
Expenses:						
Labour	3,400	3,200	(200)	12,000	9,800	(2,200)
Materials	1,100	800	(300)	2,500	2,400	(100)
Selling	50	220	170	150	800	650
Fixed	1,900	2,000	100	5,800	6,000	200
Total	6,450	6,220	(230)	20,450	19,000	(1,450)

Figure 45   *Budgetary control report (flexible budget)*

Table 14

Cost	Calculation
Direct labour	*(i)* Total operative hours x rate per hour *(ii)* Proportion of supervisor's and manager's salaries which can directly be attributed to job
Holiday allowance	A percentage of direct labour costs, typically 8 to 10%
Statutory payments	A percentage of direct labour costs, approximately 13%
Materials and equipment	8 to 10% of direct labour costs for a labour-intensive service
Consumables	Likely usage of all items determined and costed
Capital	A percentage of the annual depreciation determined by the proportion of the equipment total working time spent on a job
Spares, servicing, repairs	Actual costs forecasted, but can typically be about 1% of direct labour costs
Indirect costs (overheads)	A percentage of the total direct costs governed by the total activity level of the organization. For example, if the total indirect costs of an organization are predicted to be £100,000 and the direct costs £1,000,000, to recover the indirect costs 10%* of the direct costs of each job must be added to the direct costs
Profit	A percentage of the total direct and indirect costs governed by level of activity and market forces
VAT	At prevailing rates

*That is, [(100,000/1,000,000) × 100%]

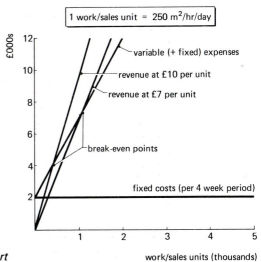

Figure 46 *Example of a break-even chart*

Direct labour	£
Operatives (1,000 hr at £1.50/hr)	1,500
Supervision (4% of supervisor's salary at £4,000 p.a.)	160
	1,660
Holidays (8% of direct labour)	133
Statutory payments (13% of direct labour)	216
Materials and equipment (vacuum cleaner at £200 depreciated over five years and used for no other purpose)	40
Spares, etc. (predicted expenditure)	15
Contracted services (deep cleaning of carpet once p.a.)	200
	2,264
Overheads (15% of total direct costs at £2,264)	340
	2,604
Profit (at 10% of total direct and indirect costs)	260
	2,864
VAT (at 15%)	430
Total cost of service	£2,604
Selling price of service	£2,864 + VAT

Break-even charts When an essentially similar type of service is being provided for a number of consumers and it can be broken down into recognizable units, break-even charts can be used. A chart will give an indication of the price at which a service must be sold at different levels of activity in order to break even (expenditure = revenue) and will highlight the situation where the level of activity is falling below that at which all expenses can be recovered at a particular selling price. Figure 46 shows a typical chart and shows, per four-week period:

1 Cost of units produced, e.g. 2,000 units, £12,500.
2 Revenue produced by selling those units, e.g. 2,000 units at £7 = £14,000.
3 Number of units to be sold at a particular price to break even, e.g. at £7 the number of units to be sold will be 1,000.
4 The difference between expenditure and revenue at different levels of activity, e.g. if only 500 units are sold at £7 per unit, the deficit will be £1,400.

Estimating from floor areas and total hourly cost If the total operating costs (direct and indirect) and the total number of operating hours can be determined or predicted for an organization or department, then an hourly cost can be determined. For example:

Total operating cost	£600,000
Total number of operating hours, direct labour	100,000
Cost per hour	£6.00

This figure can be used to estimate costs of producing a particular service. An organization might divide buildings or parts of a building into a number of broad classifications. For example:

Type of area	Daily rate, m²/hr (cost/m²/day)	
	Light furniture	Dense furniture
Largely carpeted	250 m²/hr (2.4p)	200 m²/hr (3.0p)
Uncarpeted (light soil)	200 m²/hr (3.0p)	150 m²/hr (4.0p)
Uncarpeted (heavy soil)	175 m²/hr (3.43p)	125 m²/hr (4.8p)

Assuming a cost per hour of £6.00, if the cost per hour in each classification is divided by the daily work rate, this produces the price to clean 1 m² of floor per day, the figure to be used in future estimating, i.e.

600p/250 m²/hr = 2.4p/m²/day

For example, if a building of 1,000 m² is mainly carpeted with dense furniture, the estimated costs would be:

Per day	1,000 m² × 3.0p =	£30.00
Per week (5 days)	£30 × 5	= £150.00
Per annum (250 days)	£30 × 250	= £7,500

To the estimated cost will be added a percentage for profit and VAT, if appropriate. It should be appreciated that this method of costing only gives an 'average' cost and is not a substitute for accurate costing.

An alternative approach is to devise costs per square metre for particular types of location by reference to similar jobs already carried out. As before, and allowing for changes in circumstances, such figures will only be an approximate estimate.

Warning Absorption costing techniques can result in difficulties when activity levels differ significantly from budget. A reduction in activity can result in a failure to recover fixed overheads while an increase can result in estimates being less competitive than they might otherwise be.

Cost/quality control

The provision of cleaning, accommodation or maintenance services is an annually recurring expense and one that is usually rising. It is impossible to completely separate quality and cost since the two are interdependent, i.e.

Quality = Essential tasks × Frequency
Cost   = Task performed × Frequency × Cost per performance

This is often expressed as:

Cost   = Time consumed × Wages per unit of time

although this is an over simplification.

Quality/cost control systems should involve the most effective utilization of resources – labour, equipment and materials – in order to break-even in institutional establishments or to maximize profits in commercial organizations.

Control = Maximization + Efficient use of resources to provide a service meeting consumer requirements

A high level of control demands the formulation of organizational policy, i.e. budgets, work planning, security, effective purchasing, storage and issue of materials and equipment. A good control system does not necessarily entail a great deal of clerical work, but must be designed to suit the requirements of each individual organization.

Stock control

Effective stock control can significantly reduce the costs involved in the provision of cleaning and other services. It will involve the purchase, receipt, storage, issue, security and monitoring of the utilization and consumption of equipment and materials.

Purchasing

The initial stages of a sound purchasing policy are to determine quality and cost guidelines, usually called specifications. (An example is shown in Figure 47.) These guidelines must be realistic and so should be reviewed periodically to ensure that they meet the needs of the department. A well planned purchasing policy should ensure that:

- Specifications are adhered to.
- Materials and equipment are purchased to anticipate needs.
- Prices are competitive.
- Haphazard buying does not occur.
- Advantage may be taken of special offers.
- Bulk purchases at reduced prices may be made, where there is adequate, secure storage space available.

Many large organizations, e.g. large hotel groups and local authorities, have adopted a central purchasing policy, whereby a supplies department, in consultation with users, determines cost and quality of materials and equipment to be purchased and can negotiate favourable prices from suppliers because it is a major purchasing power. This method of purchasing should promote standardization of materials and equipment throughout the organization at the most competitive prices.

Receipt of stores

It is of vital importance that goods being delivered

Supplier: **National Bedding Co.**

Address:

XYZ Hotel Group

Specification No: **51372**

Item: Bedspread – Single size

Construction: 'Candlewick'

Fibre content: 100% cotton

Colour: White

Height of pile: 1 cm.

Design: Heavily embossed

Performance: Samples of 1 complete item, plus fabric samples to be submitted for testing: abrasion, laundry, strength of construction, wear.

Specification prepared by: K. Smith

Date: 20/12/81

Figure 47 *Example of a purchasing specification*

Date	Supplier	Order number	Delivery note number	Goods	Number	Unit	Quality	Received by
1.6.81	D.M.Brown	001736	958143	Bars toilet soap	6	Case(24)	✓	M Smith
1.6.81	"	"	"	Bars scrubbing soap	3	Case(24)	✓	M Smith
1.6.81	"	"	"	Toilet rolls	6	Case(24)	✓	M Smith
1.6.81	"	"	"	Toilet tissue	1	Case(36)	✓	M Smith
1.6.81	"	"	"	Rubber gloves	1	Box (12 pairs small)	✓	M Smith
					1	box (12 pairs med.)	✓	M Smith
					1	box (12 pairs large)	✓	M Smith

Figure 48 *Example of part of a goods-received book*

are carefully checked against the specification for quantity, quality and any damage in transit. Where possible it is preferable to arrange deliveries at quiet periods of the working day so that everything may be checked thoroughly. Records should be made of all goods received before transporting to stores.

Records

All goods received should be entered in a goods-received book. It may be a book, sheets or involve the use of a computer and suitable software package (see Figure 48). Specific records are normally kept for consumable goods, e.g. cleaning agents, and non-consumable goods, e.g. linen and cleaning machines.

For each type of equipment or materials a record should be made detailing all relevant information. Figures 49 and 50 show two possible ways of recording relevant information for consumable items. Figure 51 shows the essential information to be recorded for mechanical equipment, in this case a cleaning machine. Figure 52 shows a typical linen stock sheet and Figure 153 a laundry list.

Storage

The storage of linen is described in Volume 1. In this section we are principally concerned with cleaning equipment and materials. Unless storage facilities are of adequate size for handling and storage of items required, wastage and inefficiency may occur. The main requirements for correct storage of goods are:

- Each item should be stored in a specific place.
- Those items most frequently used, should be most accessible, i.e. near the door and easily reached.
- Stock should be stored so that it can be used in rotation.
- Details of date of receipt and shelf-life for each new delivery should be recorded.
- Storage areas must be secure.
- Access to stores should be strictly controlled. Stable-type doors are helpful in preventing access to all grades of staff.

Item: **Rubber gloves · heavy duty**

Supplier: **Planters Ltd.**

Minimum stock level: **10 pairs**

Date	Receipts	Cost per item	Issued number	To:	Stock in hand
31·5·81	-	-	·	-	15
1·6·81	15	£0·45	1	Mrs Jones	29
8·6·81	-	-	2	Mrs Smith	27
15·6·81	-	-	8	Floor Team A	19
22·6·81	-	-	8	Floor Team b	11
29·6·81	15	£0·47	-	-	26

Figure 49 *Example of a stock sheet for consumable goods (1)*

Material: **Furniture Cream**

Manufacturer: **Furnipol Ltd**

Supplier: **Kleenails**

Unit: **Case - 24 jars**

Minimum stock level: **4 cases**

Date	Opening stock	Receipts	Total	Issued numbers	Area	Total
1.1.81	5 cases (120 jars)	4 cases (96 jars)	9 jars (216 jars)	12 jars	A	8½ cases (204 jars)
1.2.81	8½ cases (204 jars)	-	8½ cases (204 jars)	12 jars / 12 jars	B / C	7½ cases (180 jars)
1.3.81	7½ cases (180 jars)	-	7½ cases (180 jars)	24 jars / 24 jars	D / E	5½ cases (132 jars)
1.4.81	5½ cases (132 jars)	-	5½ cases (132 jars)	12 jars / 12 jars	F / G	4 cases (96 jars)
1.5.81	4 cases (96 jars)	4 cases (96 jars)	8 cases (192 jars)	12 jars	A	7½ cases (180 jars)

Figure 50 *Example of a stock sheet for consumable goods (2)*

Name of machine: Super Cleanit 7	
Name of manufacturer: Cleanall Ltd.	Name of supplier: Cleaning Supplies Ltd.
Serial number: AH/YR3/8651	
Date of purchase: 1.5.81	Department code number: A7/3/57
Period of guarantee: Motor - 2 years all other parts - 1 year	Cost: £285.00 complete
Date first issued: 1.6.81	Location: Dept. M

Tools and accessories purchased	Date	Cost
Carpet kit	1.5.81	included in initial cost
Upholstery kit	1.5.81	included in initial cost
High dusting kit	1.11.81	£65.00
Metal burnishing kit	1.5.82	£85.00
Venetian blind kit	1.11.82	£45.00

Maintenance/spare parts	Date	Cost
Complete service	1.11.81	under guarantee
Complete service	1.5.82	under guarantee
Motor service	1.11.82	under guarantee
Motor service	1.5.83	under guarantee
Complete service	1.5.84	£35.00
Flexible hose	1.5.84	£24.00
Fan belt	1.5.84	£0.60
Carrying handle	1.5.84	£6.50

Figure 51 *Example of a record card for mechanical equipment*

Location: **XYZ Hotel**			Date: **1.5.81**				
Stock item	New stock		Stock written off			Total stock in hand	
	No.	Date	No.	Date	Reason	No.	Date
Sheets: linen double	10	1.5.81	12	1.5.81	badly stained	48	1.5.81
linen single	50	1.5.81	8	1.5.81	torn and stained beyond repair	268	1.5.81
linen cot			1	1.5.81	torn beyond repair	9	1.5.81

Figure 52 *Example of a linen stock sheet*

Location: **XYZ Hotel Newtown**			Date: **5.5.81**
Stock item	No. despatched	No. returned	Comments
Sheets: linen single	94	93	1 remaining at laundry- stain removal
Sheets: linen double	10	10	-
Sheets: linen cot	6	7	Sheet missing since 1.4.81 returned.

Figure 53 *Example of a laundry list*

- Temperature should be carefully controlled in storage areas to prevent deterioration of some cleaning agents.
- Adequate lighting and ventilation must be provided.
- Flammable items must be stored under special conditions.

It is important that all storage facilities for cleaning equipment and materials are well planned. Ideally, there should be a cleaners' or room attendants' store (often known as HMC) adjacent to each area of work, a small bulk storeroom for small equipment and materials and a machine repair and storage area. In some

establishments, machinery belongs to a central pool and is issued to each area when necessary. Where this is the case, it is preferable to have a separate room for machines currently in use, and a second storeroom for new machines and those awaiting repair. Also the individual cleaner's store can be reduced in size, as there will be no necessity to accommodate such large items. The requirements of the various storage areas are described below.

A cleaner's store should contain:

One bucket sink and one ordinary sink with hot and cold water and detergent supply.
Adequate lighting and ventilation.
Electric socket.
Wall rack for large manual equipment and machine accessories.
Cupboard with work top.
Shelves for materials.
Door fitted with lip to prevent leakages running into the main area of the building.
Hanging or floor space for vacuum cleaner.
Waste bins.

A small store for manual equipment and bulk materials This general storage area should be secure and sited in an area convenient for despatch of stores to all areas of the building. It should contain:

One sink with hot and cold water and detergent dispenser.
One floor gully.
Shelves for small equipment and materials.
Adequate lighting and ventilation.
Electric socket.
Wall racks for large manual equipment.
Waste bins.
Work top and seat.
Files for stock records.
Door lip to prevent leakages running into the main area of the building.

The machine room should be secure and should contain:

Two views of a store for bulk materials

One sink with hot and cold water and detergent dispenser.

One floor gully.

Adequate lighting and ventilation.

Electric sockets.

Waste bins.

Floor area divided into bays and numbered for each type of machine.

Drawers and cupboards for accessories and spares.

Work top.

Record card in each bay for each item of equipment.

Where there is a separate machine repair room, it should be adjacent to the machine room and should contain the facilities listed for the machine room with extra work benches and floor space for machine repairs. Alternatively, one room may serve both of these functions.

Security of stores

The provision of a security system for all stores is essential and the following points must be considered. Where it is necessary to provide an emergency stock, e.g. linen for unexpected hotel guests, this should be provided in a special store cupboard. Staff should not be allowed access to the main stores and a simple record of issue must be kept. All storage cupboards should have suitable locks and security devices. Accessibility of keys should be strictly limited. All keys should be signed in and out. Master keys should always be in the possession of the senior member of staff on duty.

The issue and distribution of stores

Ideally stores should be issued periodically, e.g. once per week or once per month, and not on a daily basis. A procedure for the issue of stores should be laid down and adhered to except in times of emergency.

The stores will usually be distributed either by staff collecting their stock or by storekeepers or supervisors delivering it to them. When staff are to collect their own stores, it is helpful if each member of staff fills in an order form which is then left with the storekeeper. Staff return to collect their completed order later in the day and provide evidence of the need for new items of small equipment, e.g. torn rubber gloves.

When stores are delivered to each area, department or ward, a 'topping up' system is generally used. Stock levels are set for each type of equipment or material used. The level will be determined by the usage, frequency of topping up and any additional amount to allow for emergencies. The storekeeper should restock each area to the agreed levels periodically and record the stores issued. Requirements for additional stocks before restocking is due must be investigated and not complied with automatically. Details of stores issued should be recorded on the appropriate stock cards or sheets (see Figures 49 and 50). When minimum stock levels of a particular item are reached it must be reordered from the supplier.

Monitoring of materials and equipment consumption

In order to monitor the consumption of materials

and equipment by any area or department, goods issued to each area can be recorded (see Figure 54). This allows the length of time stock lasts in each department to be followed and will highlight excessive usage.

Stocktaking

It is important to take stock regularly to ensure that stock-in-hand actually equals stock-on-record. Any discrepancies arising should be accounted for and record cards or sheets amended accordingly.

When stocktaking, pro-forma stocktaking sheets should be used which, where possible, follow the order of goods on the shelves. A check that stock is being rotated should also be made.

Stocktaking will help to reduce the cost of equipment and materials. It will:

- Highlight stock discrepancies, so promoting investigation.
- Act as a deterrent, staff being less tempted to pilfer if stock is checked regularly.
- Ensure that stock is used in the correct sequence and not kept beyond its shelf life.
- Provide a set of statistics that will highlight unpopular slow moving stocks.

The procedure for checking linen stocks provides a typical example.

Linen stocktaking

Using pro-forma sheets (see Figure 55) checks should be made of each department holding linen stocks and for the whole establishment. The actual stock for each department and for the whole establishment is compared with the estbalishment stock for the department and with the total stock in hand for the establishment including any stock at the laundry.

The utilization of cleaning materials and equipment

Accommodation services staff must be trained to use cleaning materials and equipment efficiently and to take all due care to prevent wastage.

Materials and equipment issues

Area: A Floor Date	Dusters	Scrim	Mutton cloth	Floor cloth	Mop head	Stock	Dust control mop	+ holder	Bucket	Rubber gloves	Squeegee	Bucket	Abrasive pad	Detergent	Toilet roll	Toilet soap	Acid cleaners	Abrasive cream	Furniture polish
1.1.81	1				1		1	1						1	6	6	1	1	1
8.1.81		1		1										1	6	6	1	1	1
15.1.81			1				1	1						1	6	6	1	1	1
22.1.81	1									1				1	6	6	1	1	1
29.1.81					1		1	1					1	1	6	6	1	1	1

Figure 54   *Example of a stock consumption form*

Location: XYZ Hotel Newtown			Date: 1.5.81		
Stock item	Established stock/ stock in hand	Actual stock	Stock at laundry	Loss/ gain	Comments
Sheets: linen single	268	158	93	-17	Check with laundry and recheck figures
Sheets: linen double	48	40	10	+2	check previous stock figures
Sheets: linen cot	9	2	7	0	

Figure 55   *Example of a linen stocktaking sheet*

Supervisors must control the use of materials and equipment and monitor its use in their daily routines. Wastage can often be detected by physical observation and by analysis of stock records. Inspection of individual cleaners' cupboards may reveal 'hoarding' of materials.

It is of particular importance to be aware that small high-cost items of equipment and materials need extra control to prevent losses occurring.

Planned maintenance and servicing programmes will help to ensure effective utilization of large equipment.

Summary

The importance of stock control procedures cannot be too highly stressed, since they provide the following benefits:

- A regular supply of the correct materials and equipment to enable work to be carried out efficiently.
- The correct levels of stock in storage at any given time, too much stock consuming available resources of money and space.
- Highlighting of wastage, possibly due to pilferage, incorrect use of materials or need for further training.

- Simplification of the requisitioning of new stock.
- A basis for comparing efficiency.

Building security

Staff will often be on duty at times when there is little activity within the building and will require keys for access to work areas. It is essential that supervisors inculcate awareness of the need for security in staff from the first day of employment, stressing:

- The security and care of keys.
- The importance of unlocking those rooms necessary for cleaning and of securing them before moving on to the next section of work.
- The care of the personal property of the building's occupants.
- The care of their own personal property.
- The care and security of equipment and materials.
- The need for vigilance and reporting of unauthorized personnel in any area.
- The immediate reporting of faulty locks, window catches, etc.
- The immediate reporting of loss or breakages.
- The maintenance of confidentiality, particularly papers and documents where applicable.
- The importance of checking the authorization of all personnel requiring access to rooms, e.g. workmen, deliverymen, guests who have lost keys.
- The immediate reporting of any unusual occurrence.
- The need for checking that a building is completely secure when it is vacated.
- That all naked lights and flames be extinguished when leaving the building.
- That equipment left on should not be turned off without checking first.

Other aspects related to the security of a building will include the following:

- Night security lights in unattended buildings.
- Bars and other devices fitted to ground-floor windows.
- A secure place, e.g. a safe, provided for cash and valuable items.
- Cleaning staff may have a primary responsibility for security in some buildings.
- Identity cards issued to authorized personnel.

The key suite

As the care of keys is so important, it is necessary to understand the key systems and know the use of each type of key.

Individual room keys are issued to the person using the room, e.g. hotel guest or secretary. This key will be numbered or tagged to identify the door which it will open. This type of key will only open one lock.

In an hotel, the guests should hand in keys each time they go out, so that the key may be placed on a key board. This board should be out of sight of the general public, as a further security measure.

Where individual room keys are issued to members of staff to allow access to their work place, there should be a definite security policy, e.g. authorization given to one member of staff in each work area to collect, carry and return keys to the security officer. A deputy should also be nominated to take over this responsibility during the absence of the authorized person.

Many modern room locks incorporate a catch which the occupant of the room may operate to provide greater privacy, e.g. to prevent entry of a hotel chambermaid. The grand master key, described below, overrides this catch and will open the door.

Sub-master keys will normally be carried by the staff carrying out the cleaning and servicing of rooms. A sub-master key opens all the rooms in one area, e.g. a floor of an hotel or a suite of offices, and relieves the member of staff of the necessity to carry individual room keys. The sub-master key will be collected from and returned to the accommodation or cleaning services supervisor for that area of work.

Master keys will usually be held by the most senior member of the accommodation and cleaning services staff. Master keys will open all rooms in a building and so must be carried conscientiously.

Grand master keys are usually held by a senior member of staff in each organization, e.g. either the duty manager or the executive head housekeeper in an hotel, or the hospital administrator in a hospital. The grand master key will open all rooms in a building, but will also double-lock any room so that no other key in the suite can unlock it. This may be necessary for greater security of confidential material, to prevent access to an area whilst in need of repair or for any other reason when it is preferable to prevent the entry of staff, guests or visitors into an area.

Cash and valuables

Most establishments will have a safe or safe deposit boxes where guests, patients or residents can deposit valuable belongings. The availability of this service should be made known to all residents, who should be encouraged to make use of it. The service can be advertised in brochures. leaflets and notices left in each room.

Staff should be positively discouraged from bringing valuables to work. The induction programme could usefully include this point, which should be emphasized regularly. If it is impossible for a member of staff to leave valuables at home, then secure storage should be provided in the safe or safety deposit box throughout the hours of duty. This point should also be emphasized during staff training sessions.

Lost property

If a member of staff finds any lost property in the area being serviced, e.g. when servicing a bedroom after the resident has moved out, it should be handed immediately to the accommodation or cleaning services supervisor for that area. The supervisor should then follow the procedure laid down by the organization for the processing of lost property. This will usually involve the following stages:

1 The details and description of the goods are entered in a lost property book.
2 The goods are labelled and sometimes wrapped.
3 The goods are kept in a secure place for six months.
4 An attempt should be made to trace the owner. If the owner is still in the building it should be fairly easy to contact him, otherwise it may be necessary to write to him. In either case, the probable owner of the goods should not be given a full description of the property.
5 When the owner claims the goods, the lost property should not be handed over until the claimant can show that he is the real owner. Staff, when dealing with claimants of lost property, must exercise diplomacy.

Recruitment of staff

The careful recruitment and selection of accommodation and cleaning services staff can contribute to total building security if the departmental manager tries to establish that prospective employees are both honest and security-conscious. References and reports from previous employers may assist in this matter.

Once staff have been employed the need for security must be stressed in all training programmes and security training must be carried out regularly.

Index